SEXUAL HEALING IN THE CONFINES OF MARRIAGE

SONG OF SOLOMON

Rev. Anthony Martin

Author-Inspirational/Motivational

Evangelistic Speaker

THE KINGDOM CULTURE FELLOWSHIP MINISTRIES

&

CHRISTAIN SELF PUBLISHING CO

SEXUAL HEALING IN THE CONFINES OF MARRIAGE
THE SONG OF SOLOMON
By Rev. Anthony Martin

Printed in the United States of America

Copyright © 2015; 2016

ISBN 978-1-63273-017-6

Unless otherwise indicated, Bible quotations are taken from

All rights reserved solely by the author. The author guarantees all contents are original and do not infringe upon the legal rights of any other person or work. No part of this book may be reproduced in any form without the permission of the author. The views expressed in this book are not necessarily those of the publisher.

Unless otherwise indicated, Bible quotations are taken from The Kingdom Culture Exploratory Study Bible, The Kingdom English Standard Bible. (TKESB)

The Kingdom Culture Fellowship Ministries
& Christian Self Publishing Co.

www.thekingdomcultureblog.com

Contents

Preface iv

Introduction v

1. The Purpose For A Husband 8
2. The Purpose For A Wife 22
3. The Purpose For Sex 39
4. The Purpose for Marriage 45
5. The Song of Solomon 55

A Message from the Pastor's Desk

This Book is Dedicated

THE
HIGHEST
FORM
OF
GLORIFYING
GOD

INTRODUCTION

The Song of Solomon called in the Vulgate and Septuagint, "The Song of Songs," from the opening words. This title denotes its superior excellence, according to the Hebrew idiom; so holy of holies, equivalent to "most holy" (Ex 29:37); the heaven of heavens, equivalent to the highest heavens (De 10:14). It is one of the five volumes (megilloth) placed immediately after the Pentateuch in manuscripts of the Jewish Scriptures. It is also fourth of the Hagiographa (Cetubim, writings) or the third division of the Old Testament, the other two being the Law and the Prophets. The Jewish enumeration of the Cetubim is Psalms, Proverbs, Job, Canticles, Ruth, Lamentations, Ecclesiastes, Esther, Daniel, Ezra (including Nehemiah), and Chronicles. Its canonicity is certain; it is found in all Hebrew manuscripts of Scripture; also in the Greek Septuagint; in the catalogues of Melito, bishop of Sardis, A.D. 170 (Eusebius, Ecclesiastical History, 4.26), and of others of the ancient Church. Origen and Jerome tell us that the Jews forbade it to be read by any until he was thirty years old. It certainly needs a degree of spiritual maturity to enter right into the holy mystery of love which it allegorically sets forth. To such as have attained this maturity, of whatever age they be, the Song of Songs is one of the most edifying of the sacred writings. Rosenmuller justly says; the sudden transitions of the bride from the court to the grove are inexplicable, on the supposition that it describes merely human love. Had it been the latter, it would have been positively objectionable, and never would have been inserted in the holy canon.

INTRODUCTION

The allusion to "Pharaoh's chariots" (So 1:9) has been made a ground for conjecturing that the love of Solomon and Pharaoh's daughter is the subject of the Song. But this passage alludes to a remarkable event in the history of the Old Testament Church, the deliverance from the hosts and chariots of Pharaoh at the Red Sea. (However, see So. 1:9). The other allusions are quite opposed to the notion; the bride is represented at times as a shepherdess (So 1:7), "an abomination to the Egyptians" (Ge. 46:34); so also So. 1:6; 3:4; 4:8; 5:7 are at variance with it. The Christian fathers, Origen and Theodore, compared the teachings of Solomon to a ladder with three steps; Ecclesiastes, natural (the nature of sensible things, vain); Proverbs, moral; Canticles, mystical (figuring the union of Christ and the Church). The Jews compared Proverbs to the outer court of Solomon's temple, Ecclesiastes to the holy place, and Canticles to the holy of holies. Understood allegorically, the Song is cleared of all difficulty. "Shulamith" (So 6:13), the bride, is thus an appropriate name, Daughter of Peace being the feminine of Solomon, equivalent to the Prince of Peace. She by turns is a vinedresser, shepherdess, midnight inquirer, and prince's consort and daughter, and He a suppliant drenched with night dews, and a king in His palace, in harmony with the various relations of the Church and Christ. As Ecclesiastes sets forth the vanity of love of the creature, Canticles sets forth the fullness of the love which joins believers and the Savior.

INTRODUCTION

The entire economy of salvation, one says, aims at restoring to the world the lost spirit of love. God is love, and Christ is the embodiment of the love of God. As the other books of Scripture present severally their own aspects of divine truth, so Canticles furnishes the believer with language of holy love, wherewith his heart can commune with his Lord; and it portrays the intensity of Christ's love to him; the affection of love was created in man to be a transcript of the divine love, and the Song clothes the latter in words; were it not for this, we should be at a loss for language, having the divine warrant, wherewith to express, without presumption, the fervor of the love between Christ and us. The image of a bride, a bridegroom, and a marriage, to represent this spiritual union, has the sanction of Scripture throughout; nay, the spiritual union was the original fact in the mind of God, of which marriage is the transcript (Isa 54:5; 62:5; Jer. 3:1, &c.; Ezek. 16:1-63; 23:1-49; Mt 9:15; 22:2; 25:1, &c.; Jn. 3:29; 2Co 11:2; Eph 5:23-32, where Paul does not go from the marriage relation to the union of Christ and the Church as if the former were the first; but comes down from the latter as the first and best recognized fact on which the relation of marriage is based; Re 19:7; 21:2; 22:17). Above all, the Song seems to correspond to, and form a trilogy with, Psalms 45 and 72, which contain the same imagery; just as Psalm 37 answers to Proverbs, and the Psalms 39 and 73 to Job. Love to Christ is the strongest, as it is the purest, of human passions, and therefore needs the strongest language to express it: to the pure in heart the phraseology, drawn from the rich imagery of Oriental poetry, will not only appear not indelicate or exaggerated, but even below the reality.

CHAPTER I

The Purpose For A Husband

The apostle tells the Corinthians that it was good, in that juncture of time, for Christians to keep themselves single. Yet he says that marriage, and the comforts of that state, are settled by Divine wisdom. Though none may break the law of God, yet that perfect rule leaves men at liberty to serve him in the way most suited to their powers and circumstances, of which others often are very unfit judges. All must determine for themselves, seeking counsel from God how they ought to act. .Let the husband ... - "Let them not imagine that there is any virtue in bring separate from each other, as if they were in a state of celibacy". They are bound to each other; in every way they are to evince kindness, and to seek to promote the happiness and purity of each other. There is a great deal of delicacy used here by Paul, and his expression is removed as far as possible from the grossness of pagan writers. His meaning is plain; but instead of using a word to express it which would be indelicate and offensive, he uses one which is not indelicate in the slightest degree. The word which he uses εὔνοιαν eunoian," benevolence" denotes kindness, good-will, affection of mind. And by the use of the word "due" ὀφειλομένην opheilomenēn, he reminds them of the sacredness of their vow, and of the fact that in person, property, and in every respect, they belong to each other. It was necessary to give this direction, for the contrary might have been regarded as proper by many who would have supposed there was special virtue and merit in living separate from each other; as facts have shown

Sexual Healing In the Confines of Marriage

that many have imbibed such an idea - and it was not possible to give the rule with more delicacy than Paul has done. Many, however, instead of "due benevolence," read ὀφειλὴν opheilēn, "a debt, or that which is owed;" and this reading has been adopted, with a delicacy not unlike the apostle Paul, uses the word φιλότητα filotēta, "friendship," to express the same idea. Let the husband render to the wife due benevolence, The Syriac version renders it, , "due love"; and so the Arabic; and may include all the offices of love, tenderness, humanity, care, provision, and protection, which are to be performed by the husband to his wife; though it seems chiefly, if not solely, here to respect what is called, Exodus 21:10 "her marriage duty", as distinct from food and raiment to be allowed her; and what is meant by it the Jewish doctors will tell us: one says (t), it is , "the use of the marriage bed"; and, says another (u), , "it is to lie with her", according to the way of all the earth. And so the phrase here, "due benevolence", is a euphemism, and designs the act of coition; which as it is an act of love and affection, a sign of mutual benevolence, so of justice; it is a due debt from divine ordination, and the matrimonial contract. The Jewish doctors have fixed and settled various canons (w) concerning the performance, of this conjugal debt: and the apostle may not be altogether without some view to the rules and customs which obtained in his own nation. And, likewise also the wife unto the husband; she is not to refuse the use of the bed when required, unless there is some just impediment, otherwise she comes under the name of a "rebellious

The Purpose For A Husband

wife"; concerning whom, and her punishment, the Jews (x) give the following rules: "a woman that restrains her husband from the use of the bed, is called rebellious; and when they ask her why she rebels, if she says, because it is loathsome to me, and I cannot lay with him; then they oblige him to put her away directly, without her dowry; and she may not take anything of her husband's, not even her shoe strings, nor her hair lace; but what her husband did not give her she may take, and go away: and if she rebels against her husband, on purpose to afflict him, and she does to him so or so, and despises him, they send to her from the sanhedrim, and say to her, know you, that if you continue in your rebellion, you shall not prosper? and after that they publish her in the synagogues and schools four weeks, one after another, and say, such an one has rebelled against her husband; and after the publication, they send and say to her, if you continue in thy rebellion, you will lose your dowry; and they appoint her twelve months, and she has no sustenance from her husband all that time; and she goes out at the end of twelve months without her dowry, and returns everything that is her husband's." Defraud not one the other; that is: Withhold not yourselves one from another; which he rightly calls defrauding one another, because he had before declared it a debt; and further declared, that neither the husband nor the wife had a power over their own bodies, but the power of either of their bodies was in their correlate.

He adds, except it be with consent, mutual consent, and then it is indeed no defrauding; and for a time, for a religious end, that they might give themselves to fasting and prayer: not that this abstinence is necessary to us by any Divine precept, to prepare us for solemn prayer, (for such only is here spoken of), for then the apostle would not have made consent necessary in this case; but the Jews were commanded it, Exodus 19:15, as a preparation to their hearing of the law; and it was a piece of the legal purification, as appeared from 1 Samuel 21:4, as to which Christians were at liberty, and might observe or not observe it, as they agreed. And come together again, that Satan tempt you not for your incontinency: then he requires, that they should return to their former course, not defrauding one another, lest the devil, observing their abstinence, should tempt them to unlawful mixtures, seeing their inability to contain themselves within the bounds of temperance and chastity. Do not defraud one the other ... By withholding due benevolence, denying the use of the marriage bed, refusing to pay the conjugal debt and which is called a "diminishing of her marriage duty", Exodus 21:10 where the Septuagint use the same word "defraud", as the apostle does here; it is what both have a right to, and therefore, if either party is denied, it is a piece of injustice, it is properly a defrauding; though with proper conditions, such as follow, it may be lawful for married persons to lie apart, and abstain from the use of the bed, but then it should never be done, except it be with consent:

because they have a mutual power over each other's bodies, and therefore the abstinence must be voluntary on each side; otherwise injury is done to the person that does not consent, who is deprived against will of just right; but if there is agreement, then there is no defrauding, because each give up their right; and such a voluntary abstinence is commended by the Jews (z); "everyone that lessens the use of the bed, lo, he, is praiseworthy; and he who does not make void, or, cause to cease the due benevolence, but , "by consent of his wife"; i.e. he also is praiseworthy: another condition of this abstinence is that it be only for a time; which shall be agreed unto, and fixed by both parties; not for ever which would be contrary to the will of God; the institution and end of marriage, and of dangerous consequence to either party. The Jews allow of a vow of continence for a while; and which they limit to different persons; thus (a), "if a man by a vow excludes, wife from the use of the bed, the school of Shammai say it is for the space of two weeks, the school of Hillell say one week; scholars go out to learn the law, without leave of their wives, thirty days, workmen one week;" which vow, for such a limited time, they seem to allow of, without mutual consent; and herein they disagree with the rule the apostle gives; and who further observes, the end to be had in view by such a voluntary separation for a time, that you may give yourselves to fasting and prayer; not that this was necessary for the ordinary discharge of such service, as for private acts of devotion among themselves, and constant family prayer; but either when times of fasting and prayer on some emergent occasions were appointed by themselves, or by the church, or by the civil government on account of some extraordinary and momentous affairs; and this seems to be observed by the apostle, in agreement with the customs and rules of the Jewish nation, which forbid the use of the bed, as on their great and annual fast, the day of atonement (b), so on their fasts appointed by the sanhedrim for obtaining of rain (c): the word "fasting" is omitted in the Vulgate Latin and Ethiopic versions, and so it is in the Alexandrian copy, two of Stephens's; and others: the apostle adds, and come together again; to the same bed, and the use of it, and that for this reason, that Satan tempt you not for your incontinence; for not having the gift of continence, should they pretend to keep apart long: Satan, who knows the temperament and disposition of men and women, may tempt them not only to hatred of, and quarrels with one another, but to impure lusts and desires, to fornication, adultery, and all uncleanness; a very good reason why, though abstinence from the marriage bed for a short time, by the consent of both parties, for religious purposes, may be lawful, yet ought not to be continued; since Satan may hereby get an advantage over them, and draw them into the commission of scandalous enormities. The Jews have a notion of Satan's being a tempter and of his tempting men to various sins, which they should guard against, as idolatry, so they say (d), "you may not look after idolatry, according to <u>Deuteronomy 4:19</u> and again, you must take heed lest this be a cause of it to you, "and Satan tempt you" to look after them, and do as they do:" and again (e), frequently should a man think "upon the unity of the blessed God, lest there should be anything above or below, before him or behind him, or by him, and so, "Satan tempt him", and he come into heresy." Now those that have married I charge: so these words should be rendered, the phrase being the same with that in 1 Timothy 1:3, rendered by our translators, that thou might charge some. Yet not I — Only, or not I by any new revelation, nor by mere counsel, or prudential advice, as 1 Corinthians 7:25; 1 Corinthians 7:40. But the Lord — Namely, in the first institution of marriage, Genesis 2:24; and the Lord Christ also commanded the same, Matthew 5:32; Matthew 19:6; Matthew 19:9. The Lord Jesus, during his ministry on earth, delivered many precepts of his law in the hearing of his disciples. And those which he did not deliver in person, he promised to reveal to them by the Spirit, after his departure. Therefore there is a just foundation for distinguishing the commandments which the Lord delivered in person, from those which he revealed to the apostles by the Spirit, and which they made known to the world in their sermons and writings. This distinction is not only made by Paul; it is insinuated likewise by Peter and Jude, 2 Peter 3:3, Jdgs. 1:17, where the commandments of the apostles of the Lord and Savior are mentioned, not as inferior in authority to the commandments of the Lord, (for they were all as really his commandments as those which he delivered in person,) but as different in the manner of their communication.

Sexual Healing In the Confines of Marriage

And the apostle's intention here was not, as many have imagined, to tell us in what things he was inspired, and in what not; but to show us what commandments the Lord delivered personally in his own lifetime, and what the Spirit inspired the apostles to deliver after his departure. This Paul could do with certainty; because, although he was not of the number of those who accompanied our Lord during his ministry, all the particulars of his life and doctrine were made known to him by revelation, as may be collected from 1 Corinthians 11:23; 1 Corinthians 15:3; 1 Timothy 5:18; and from many allusions to the words and actions of Christ, found in the epistles which Paul wrote before any of the gospels were published; and from his mentioning one of Christ's sayings, not recorded by any of the evangelists, Acts 20:35. Further, that the apostle's intention, in distinguishing the Lord's commandments from those he calls his own, was not to show what things he spoke by inspiration, and what not, is evident, from his adding certain circumstances, which prove that, in delivering his own commandments, or judgment, he was really inspired. Thus, when he asserted that a widow was at liberty to marry a second time, by adding, (1 Corinthians 7:40,) she is happier if she so abide, after (that is, according to) my judgment; and I think, or, I am certain that I also have the Spirit of God, he plainly asserted that he was inspired in giving that judgment or determination. Let not the wife departs from her husband — willfully leave him, on account of any disagreement between them. But if she depart — Contrary to this express prohibition, assigning, perhaps, reasons apparently necessary for it, as that her life is in danger, or the like; let her remain unmarried, or — Rather, if it may be accomplished by any submission on her part, let her be reconciled to her husband — That, if possible, they may live in such a union and harmony as the relation requires. And let not the husband put away his wife — Except for the cause of adultery; because the obligations lying on husbands and wives are mutual and equal. The apostle, after saying concerning the wife, that if she departed from her husband, she must remain unmarried, or be reconciled to him, did not think it necessary to add a similar clause respecting the husband, namely, that if he put away his wife, he must remain unmarried, or be reconciled to her. This, however, is implied in what he says concerning him. Man and wife must not separate for any other cause than what Christ allows. Divorce, at that time, was very common among both Jews and Gentiles, on very slight pretexts. Marriage is a Divine institution; and is an engagement for life, by God's appointment. We are bound, as much as in us lies, to live peaceably with all men, Ro 12:18, therefore to promote the peace and comfort of our nearest relatives, though unbelievers. It should be the labor and study of those who are married, to make each other as easy and happy as possible. Should a Christian desert a husband or wife, when there is opportunity to give the greatest proof of love? Stay and labor heartily for the conversion of thy relative. In every state and relation the Lord has called us to peace; and everything should be done to promote harmony, as far as truth and holiness will permit.

Sexual Healing In the Confines of Marriage

And to the married - This verse commences the second subject of inquiry; to wit, whether it was proper, in the existing state of things, for those who were married to continue this relation, or whether they ought to separate. The reasons why any may have supposed that it was best to separate may have been:

(1) That their troubles and persecutions might be such that they might judge it best that families should be broken up; and,

(2) Probably many supposed that it was unlawful for a Christian wife or husband to be connected at all with a pagan and an idolater.

I command, yet not I, but the Lord - Not I so much as the Lord. This injunction is not to be understood as advice merely, but as a solemn, divine command, from which you are not at liberty to depart. Paul here professes to utter the language of inspiration, and demands obedience. The express command of "the Lord" to which he refers, is probably the precept recorded in Matthew 5:32, and Matthew 19:3-10. These precepts of Christ asserted that the marriage tie was sacred and inviolable. Let not the wife depart ... - Let her not prove faithless to her marriage vows; let her not, on any pretence, desert her husband. Though she is a Christian and he is not, yet let her not seek, on that account, to be separate from him - The law of Moses did not permit a wife to divorce herself from her husband, though it was sometimes done (compare Matthew 10:12); but the Greek and Roman laws allowed it - Grotius.

The Purpose For A Husband

But Paul here refers to a formal and legal separation before the magistrates, and not to a voluntary separation, without intending to be formally divorced. The reasons for this opinion are:

(1) That such divorces were known and practiced among both Jews and pagans.

(2) it was important to settle the question whether they were to be allowed in the Christian church.

(3) the claim would be set up, probably, that it might be done. (4) the question whether a "voluntary separation" might not be proper, where one party was a Christian, and the other not, he discusses in the following verses, 1 Corinthians 7:12-17. Here, therefore, he solemnly repeats the law of Christ that divorce, under the Christian economy, was not to be in the power either of the husband or wife. 10. not I, but the Lord—(Compare 1Co 7:12, 25, 40). In ordinary cases he writes on inspired apostolic authority (1Co 14:37); but here on the direct authority of the Lord Himself (10:11, 12). In both cases alike the things written are inspired by the Spirit of God "but not all for all time, nor all on the primary truths of the faith". Let not the wife depart—literally, "be separated from." Probably the separation on either side, whether owing to the husband or to the wife, is forbidden. The apostle had spoke to the married before, but in another case, he now returned in his discourse to them again, speaking to another case, which it should seem they had put to him;

what it was is not plainly expressed, but it may easily be gathered from 1 Corinthians 7:12,13, as also from the apostle's determination in this verse: or it was this: Whether it was lawful for the husband to depart from his wife, or the wife from her husband, unless it were in the case of adultery; for though here be nothing spoken as to that case, yet it plainly must be excepted, as determined before by our Savior; but as the Jews, so the heathens amongst whom these Corinthians lived, had entertained much too mean thoughts about the marriage bond, indulging themselves in a liberty to break it for every slight cause; and it should seem by 1 Corinthians 7:12,13, it was judged by them a sufficient cause, if one of them were not converted to the faith of Christ. Now in this case, said the apostle, I command, and what I tell you is the will of God; it is not I alone who command it, but you are to look upon it as the will of God concerning you, though revealed to you by me that am the minister of God to you. Let not the wife depart from her husband; she may be divorced from her husband in case of fornication, but let her not for any other cause make a voluntary secession. And to the married I command ... To the unmarried and widows he spoke by permission, or only gave advice and counsel to remain unmarried, provided they could contain; but if not, it was advisable to marry; but to persons already in a married state, what he has to say to them is by commandment, enjoining what they are under obligation to observe, not being at liberty to do as they will: yet not I, but the Lord; not as if he took upon him the dominion over them, to make laws for them, and, in an imperious authoritative way, oblige them to obedience to them; no; what he was about to deliver, was not a law of his own enacting and obtruding, but what their Lord, their Creator, head, husband, and Redeemer, had ordered and enjoined; and this grave solemn way of speaking he makes use of, to excite their attention, command awe and reverence, make the greater impression upon their minds, and show the obligation they were under to regard what was said:

let not the wife depart from her husband; for the same law that obliges a man to cleave to his wife, obliges the wife to cleave to her husband, Genesis 2:24 and those words of Christ, "what God hath joined together, let no man put asunder", Matthew 19:6 regard the one as well as the other; and the rules he has given, forbidding divorces only in case of adultery, Matthew 5:32 are as binding upon the wife as upon the husband. The wife therefore should not depart from her husband upon every slight occasion; not on account of any quarrel, or disagreement that may arise between them; or for every instance of moroseness and inhumanity; or because of diseases and infirmities; nor even on the score of difference in religion which, by what follows, seems to be greatly the case in view. The apostle observes this, in opposition to some rules and customs which obtained among Jews and Gentiles, divorcing and separating from one another upon various accounts; not only husbands put away their wives, but wives also left their husbands: for women to put away, or leave their husbands, were not in former times allowed of among the Jews, but from other nations crept in among them; indeed if a man married one under age, and she did not like him for her husband, she might refuse him, and go away without a bill of divorce; the manner of refusal was, by saying before two witnesses, I do not like such an one for my husband, or I do not like the espousals, with which my mother or my brother espoused me, or in such like words; and sometimes a written form of refusal was given (m); but otherwise where marriage was consummated, such a departure of the wife was not allowed. Salome, the sister of Herod, is thought to be the first that introduced it, who sent a bill of divorce to Costobarus (n) her husband; and in this she was followed by Herodias, the daughter of Aristobulus, who left her husband, and married Herod Antipas (o); and it seems certain, that this practice prevailed in Christ's time, since not only such a case is supposed, Mark 10:12 but a very flagrant instance is given in the woman of Samaria, John 4:18 who had had five husbands, not in a lawful regular manner, one after another upon their respective deaths, but she had married them, and put them away one after another: and as for the Gentiles, the account the Jews (p) give of them is, that though they had "no divorces in form, they put away one another; one says, , "a man's wife might put him away", and give him the dowry:" though, according to other accounts, they had divorces in form, which, when a man put away a woman, were called, "letters of dismission"; and when a woman left her husband, , "letters of dereliction", such as Hipparchia the wife of Alcibiades gave to him (q); and a scholar (r) gives us an instance of a Christian woman, who gave her husband what the Roman senate called a divorce.

CHAPTER II

The Purpose For A Wife

Abraham's servant, as one that chose his work before his pleasure, was for hastening home. Lingering and loitering no way become a wise and good man who is faithful to his duty. As children ought not to marry without their parents' consent, so parents ought not to marry them without their own. Rebekah consented, not only to go, but to go at once. The goodness of Rebekah's character shows there was nothing wrong in her answer, though it be not agreeable to modern customs among us. We may hope that she had such an idea of the religion and godliness in the family she was to go to, as made her willing to forget her own people and her father's house. Her friends dismiss her with suitable attendants, and with hearty good wishes. They blessed Rebekah. When our relations are entering into a new condition, we ought by prayer to commend them to the blessing and grace of God. Isaac was well employed when he met Rebekah. He went out to take the advantage of a silent evening, and a solitary place, for meditation and prayer; those divine exercises by which we converse with God and our own hearts. Holy souls love retirement; it will do us good to be often alone, if rightly employed; and we are never less alone than when alone. Observe what an affectionate son Isaac was: it was about three years since his mother died, and yet he was not, till now, comforted. See also what an affectionate husband he was to his wife. Dutiful sons promise fair to be affectionate husbands; he that fills up his first station in life with honor, is likely to do the same in those that follow.

Sexual Healing In the Confines of Marriage

Isaac receives his bride. He had been at Beer-lahai-roi, the scene of the interview of Hagar with the angel of the Lord - a spot calculated to awaken thoughts of an overruling Providence. "To meditate." This is a characteristic of Isaac's retiring, contemplative mood. Abraham was the active, authoritative father; Isaac was the passive, submissive son. To meditate was to hold converse with his own thoughts, to ponder on the import of that never-to-be-forgotten scene when he was laid on the altar by a father's hand, and a ram caught in the thicket became his substitute, and to pour out his soul unto the God of his salvation. In this hour of his grave reflection comes his destined bride with her faithful escort upon his view. Rebekah lights off the camel. Doubtless the conversation by the way with the elder of Abraham's house had made her aware of their approach to the residence of her future husband. She concludes at once that this must be he, and, alighting, asks if it be. On being informed by the servant that this is his young master, she puts on the veil, which covers the head, and hangs down gracefully both behind and before. The aged servant reports the success of his mission, and presents Rebekah. Isaac brings his cousin's daughter into the apartments formerly occupied by his mother, and accepts her as his wife. The formalities of the interview, and of her presentation to Abraham as his daughter-in-law, are all untold. "And he loved her." This is the first mention of the social affections. It comes in probably because Isaac had not before seen his bride, and now felt his heart drawn toward her, when she was presented to his view. All things were evidently done in the fear of God, as became those who were to be the progenitors of the seed of promise.

The Purpose For A Wife

We have here a description of the primeval marriage. It is a simple taking of a woman for a wife before all witnesses, and with suitable feelings and expression of reverence toward God, and of desire for his blessing. It is a pure and holy relation, reaching back into the realms of innocence, and fit to be the emblem of the humble, confiding, affectionate union between the Lord and his people.

- The Death of Abraham

1. קטורה qeṭûrâh, "Qeturah, incense."

2. זמרן zîmrān, "Zimran, celebrated in song." יקשן yāqshān, "Joqshan, fowler." מדן medān, "Medan, judge." מדין mîdyān, "Midian, one who measures." לאבק yîshbāq, "Jishbaq, he leaves." שוח shûach, "Shuach, pit."

3. לטושם leṭûshîym, "Letushim, hammered, sharpened." לאמים le'umîym, "Leummim, peoples."

4. עיפה ʿêypâh, "'Ephah, darkness." עפר ʿêper, "'Epher, dust." אבידע ʾăbîydāʿ, "Abida', father of knowledge." אלדעה ʾeldāʿâh, "Elda'ah, knowing?"

Another family is born to Abraham by Keturah, and portioned off, after which he dies and is buried.

Sexual Healing In the Confines of Marriage

And Isaac brought her into his mother's ... tent—thus establishing her at once in the rights and honors of a wife before he had seen her features. Disappointments often take place, but when Isaac saw his wife, "he loved her" and he loved her; as a man ought to love his wife, even as his own body, Ephesians 5:28; and she was a person to be beloved, being very fair, and of a goodly countenance, Genesis 24:16. The Jews say (z) she was but fourteen years of age at this time. Isaac brought her into his mother Sarah's tent, partly to give her possession of it, and partly to consummate the marriage. Women then had their tents apart from men. Genesis 18:10 24:67 31:33. Isaac was comforted after his mother's death; a sorrowful sense where of he yet had retained, though she died three years before this time. and Isaac was comforted after his mother's death; Genesis 25:20; and had made such impressions upon his spirit, that at times he was very sorrowful, and much distressed on that account; but now being blessed with so agreeable a yokefellow, his sorrow for his mother subsided, and he became cheerful and comfortable.

The Purpose For A Wife

The duty of wives is submission to their husbands in the Lord, which includes honoring and obeying them, from a principle of love to them. The duty of husbands is to love their wives. The love of Christ to the church is an example, which is sincere, pure, and constant, notwithstanding her failures. Christ gave himself for the church, that he might sanctify it in this world, and glorify it in the next, that he might bestow on all his members a principle of holiness, and deliver them from the guilt, the pollution, and the dominion of sin, by those influences of the Holy Spirit, of which baptismal water was the outward sign. The church and believers will not be without spot or wrinkle till they come to glory. But those only who are sanctified now, shall be glorified hereafter. The words of Adam, mentioned by the apostle, are spoken literally of marriage; but they have also a hidden sense in them, relating to the union between Christ and his church. It was a kind of type, as having resemblance. There will be failures and defects on both sides, in the present state of human nature, yet this does not alter the relation. All the duties of marriage are included in unity and love. And while we adore and rejoice in the condescending love of Christ, let husbands and wives learn hence their duties to each other. Thus the worst evils would be prevented, and many painful effects would be avoided.

Nevertheless - The apostle here resumes the subject which he had been discussing in Ephesians 5:21-29, and says that it was the duty of every man to love his wife as he did himself. This was the main topic, from which he had been diverted by the discussion respecting the love which the Redeemer had shown for his church. And the wife sees that she reverence her husband - The word "see" is supplied by our translators. The meaning is, that it was the special duty of the wife to show respect for her husband as the head of the family, and as set over her in the Lord; Ephesians 5:22. The word rendered "reverence," is that which usually denotes "fear" - φοβῆται phobētai. She is to fear; i. e., to honor, respect, obey the will of her husband. It is, of course, not implied that it is not also her duty to love her husband, but that there should be no usurping of authority; no disregard of the arrangement which God has made; and that order and peace should be secured in a family by regarding the husband as the source of law.

From what is here said of the duties of husband and wife we may remark:

(1) That the happiness of society depends on just views of the marriage relation. It is true the world over, that the views which prevail in regard to this relation, determine everything in reference to all other relations of life, and to all other sources of enjoyment.

(2) God designed that woman should occupy a subordinate, though an important place in the relations of social life.

The Purpose For A Wife

This arrangement is never disregarded without evils which cannot be corrected until the original intention is secured. No imaginary good that can come out of the violation of the original design; no benefits which females, individual or associated, can confer on mankind by disregarding this arrangement, can be a compensation for the evil that is done, nor can the evil be remedied unless woman occupies the place which God designed she should fill. There nothing else can supply her place; and when she is absent from that situation - no matter what good she may be doing elsewhere - there is a silent evil reigning, which can be removed only by her return. It is not hers to fight battles, or to command armies and navies, or to control kingdoms, or to make laws. Nor is it hers to go forward as a public leader even in enterprises of benevolence, or in associations designed to act on the public mind. Her empire is the domestic circle; her first influence is there; and in connection with that, in such scenes as she can engage in without trenching on the prerogative of man, or neglecting the duty which she owes to her own family.

(3) it is not best that there should be the open exercise of authority in a family. When "commands" begin in the relation of husband and wife, "happiness" flies; and the moment a husband is "disposed" to command his wife, or is "under a necessity" of doing it, that moment he may bid adieu to domestic peace and joy.

(4) a wife, therefore, should never give her husband "occasion" to command her to do anything, or forbid anything. His known wish, except in cases of conscience, should be law to her.

Sexual Healing In the Confines of Marriage

The moment she can ascertain what his will is, that moment ought to settle her mind as to what is to be done. (5) a husband should never "wish" or "expect" anything that it may not be perfectly proper for a wife to render. He, too, should consult "her" wishes; and when he understands what they are, he should regard what she prefers as the very thing which he would command. The known wish and preference of a wife, unless there be something wrong in it, should be allowed to influence his mind, and be that which he directs in the family.

(6) there is no danger that a husband will love a wife too much, provides his love be subordinate to the love of God. The command is, to love her as Christ loved the church. What love has ever been like that? How can a husband exceed it? What did not Christ endure to redeem the church? So should a husband be willing to deny himself to promote the happiness of his wife; to watch by her in sickness, and, if need be, to peril health and life to promote her welfare. Doing this, he will not go beyond what Christ did for the church. He should remember that she has a special claim of justice on him. For him she has left her father's home, forsaken the friends of her youth, endowed him with whatever property she may have, sunk her name in his, confided her honor, her character, and her happiness, to his virtue; and the least that he can do for her is to love her, and strive to make her happy. This was what she asked when she consented to become his; and a husband's love is what she still asks to sustain and cheer her in the trials of life. If she has not this, whither shall she go for comfort?

The Purpose For A Wife

(7) we may see, then, the guilt of those husbands who withhold their affections from their wives, and forsake those to whom they had solemnly pledged themselves at the altar; those who neglect to provide for their needs or to minister to them in sickness; and those who become the victims of intemperance, and leave their wives to tears. There is much, much guilt of this kind on earth. There are many, many broken vows. There are many, many hearts made to bleed. There is many a pure and virtuous woman who was once the object of tender affection, now, by no fault of hers, forsaken, abused, broken-hearted, by the brutal conduct of a husband,

(8) wives should manifest such a character as to be worthy of love. They owe this to their husbands. They demand the confidence and affection of man; and they should show that they are worthy of that confidence and affection. It is not possible to love that which is unlovely, nor to force affection where it is undeserved; and, as a wife expects that a husband will love her more than he does any other earthly being, it is but right that she should evince such a spirit as shall make that proper. A wife may easily alienate the affections of her partner in life. If she is irritable and fault-finding; if none of his ways please her; if she takes no interest in his plans, and in what he does; if she forsakes her home when she should he there, and seeks happiness abroad; or if, at home, she never greets him with a smile; if she is wasteful of his earnings, and extravagant in her habits, it will be impossible to prevent the effects of such a course of life on his mind. And when a wife perceives the slightest evidence of alienated affection in her husband, she should inquire at once whether she has not given occasion for it, and

exhibited such a spirit as tended inevitably to produce such a result. (9) to secure mutual love, therefore, it is necessary that there should be mutual kindness, and mutual loveliness of character. Whatever is seen to be offensive or painful should be at once abandoned. All the little peculiarities of temper and modes of speech that are observed to give pain should be forsaken; and, while one party should endeavor to tolerate them, and not to be offended, the other should make it a matter of conscience to remove them.

(10) the great secret of conjugal happiness is in the cultivation of a proper temper. It is not so much in the great and trying scenes of life that the strength of virtue is tested; it is in the events that are constantly occurring; the manifestation of kindness in the things that are happening every moment; the gentleness that flows along every day, like the stream that winds through the meadow and around the farm-house, noiseless but useful, diffusing fertility by day and by night. Great deeds rarely occur. The happiness of life depends little on them, but mainly on the little acts of kindness in life. We need them everywhere; we need them always. And eminently in the marriage relation there is need of gentleness and love, returning each morning, beaming in the eye, and dwelling in the heart through the livelong day.

The Purpose For A Wife

Contrast with the bride's state by nature (Isa 1:6) her state by grace (So 4:1-7), "perfect through His comeliness put upon her" (Ezek 16:14; Jn. 15:3). The praise of Jesus Christ, unlike that of the world, hurts not, but edifies; as His, not ours, is the glory (Jn. 5:44; Re 4:10, 11). Seven features of beauty are specified (So 4:1-5) ("lips" and "speech" are but one feature, So 4:3), the number for perfection. To each of these is attached a comparison from nature: the resemblances consist not so much in outward likeness, as in the combined sensations of delight produced by contemplating these natural objects doves'—the large melting eye of the Syrian dove appears especially beautiful amid the foliage of its native groves: so the bride's "eyes within her locks" (Lu 7:44). Maurer for "locks," has "veil"; but locks suit the connection better: so the Hebrew is translated (Isa 47:2). The dove was the only bird counted "clean" for sacrifice. Once the heart was "the cage of every unclean and hateful bird." Grace makes the change eyes—(Mt 6:22; Eph 1:18; contrast Mt 5:28; Eph 4:18; 1Jo 2:16). Chaste and guileless ("harmless," Mt 10:16, Margin; Jn. 1:47). John the Baptist, historically, was the "turtledove" (So 2:12), with eye directed to the coming Bridegroom: his Nazarite unshorn hair answers to "locks" (Jn. 1:29, 36) hair ... goats—The hair of goats in the East is fine like silk. As long hair is her glory, and marks her subjection to man (1Co 11:6-15), so the Nazarite's hair marked his subjection and separation unto God. (Compare Jud 16:17, with 2Co 6:17; Tit 2:14; 1Pe 2:9). Jesus Christ cares for the minutest concerns of His saints (Mt 10:30).

appear from—literally, "that lie down from"; lying along the hillside, they seem to hang from it: a picture of the bride's hanging tresses. Gilead—beyond Jordan: there stood "the heap of witness" (Ge. 31:48). Christ commended his church for her beauty, Song of Solomon 4:1-7. He called her to go with him, Song of Solomon 4:8, manifesting his love and affection for her, Song of Solomon 4:9. A further commendation of her, Song of Solomon 4:10-15. She prayed for the effectual operation of his Holy Spirit on her to make her fruitful, Song of Solomon 4:16. These and the following words are evidently spoken by the Bridegroom to and concerning his spouse. You art fair, not in thyself, but by my beauty, being clothed with my righteousness, and adorned with all the graces of my Spirit, which I acknowledge to be in you. You art fair; he repeats it, both to confirm the truth of his assertion, and to show the sincerity and fervency of his affection to her. You hast dove's eyes; you are harmless, chaste, as appears by your eyes, which commonly discover the temper of the mind or person. See more of this phrase Song of Solomon 1:15. And whereas the beauty of the spouse is here described in her several parts, we need not labor much about the application of each particular to some distinct member or grace of the church, this being the chief design of this description of a bride which is beautiful in all points, to show that completeness and absolute perfection which the church hath in part received, and shall more fully receive from Christ in the future life.

The Purpose For A Wife

Yet because the church is a body, consisting of diver's members, and enriched with variety of gifts and graces, I know no reason but the several parts of this description may have a more special regard to one or other of them. And so her eyes may here note, either, 1. Her teachers, who are instead of eyes to her, as the phrase is, Numbers 10:31, whence they are called seers and guides. 2. The disposition of her mind or heart, which is compared to the eye, Matthew 6:22, 23, and is oft discerned in the eye. Within thy locks; which being decently composed, make the eyes appear more amiable: withal this intimates the modesty of her looks; her eyes are not wanton, and wandering, or lofty, but sober, and humble, and confined within their proper bounds, looking directly upon her husband, not looking asquint upon other lovers, nor minding other Gods or Christ's. If the eyes signify teachers, the locks may note the people assembled together to hear their teachers, to whom they are a great ornament when they thrive by his teaching. Your hair; the hair of your head, which is a great ornament to the female sex, 1 Corinthians 11:15. This hair may signify either. 1. The inward thoughts and meditations; or rather, 2. The outward conversation and visible fruits of holiness, which do greatly adorn the professors and profession of religion, as hair doth the head, as is implied, 1 Timothy 2:9,10 1 Peter 3:3-5. As a flock of goats; which are comely and orderly in going, Proverbs 30:29, 31, and afford a goodly prospect.

Or rather, as the hair (which word is here to be understood, as appears both from the comparison itself, and from divers places where goats are put for goats' hair, as it is in the Hebrew text, Exodus 25:4 26:7 35:26) of a flock of goats, which in these parts was of extraordinary length, and thickness, and softness, and comeliness, and much more like to the hair of a man or woman than the hair of our goats is, as is evident both from Scripture, as Genesis 27:16 1 Samuel 19:13; and from the testimony of other ancient writers, as Apulcius, Martial. That appear from Mount Gilead; that feeding there, or coming down thence, or going up thither, show themselves evidently to those who stand below it, or near them. Or, as it is rendered in our margin, and by others, that eat, or graze of, or upon. He mentions it as a very fruitful place, and fit for the breeding of all sorts of cattle, as is manifest from Numbers 32:1 Jer. 1 19 Mich. 7:14; and especially of goats, partly because it was a hilly and woody, country, and partly because it abounded with resinous, and oily, and gummy trees, as appears from Genesis 37:25 Jeremiah 8:22 46:11, wherewith the goats are much delighted, as Dioscorides observes. And some affirm that the hair of these goats was commonly of a yellow color, as may seem probable from 1 Samuel 19:13,16, compared with 1 Samuel 16:12, and from Song of Solomon 7:5; which also was in ancient times esteemed a beauty in men or women, as the learned know. Song of Solomon 4:1-7. The Royal Suitor, King Solomon is here the speaker, and in these verses he presses his suit anew by praise of the Shulammite's beauty.

The Purpose For A Wife

The whole song is evidently modeled, as several of the succeeding songs are, on the *wasf* or description of the bride, which is so prominent a thing at marriage festivals in Syria to this day. To have established this is one theologian scholar's great merit, for until his Essay on the Threshing-Board appeared these descriptions were to a large extent inexplicable. But the discovery that the wasf is an ancient form of song connected by prescription with love and marriage explains its appearance here. In a series of love-songs disposed so as to give scenes of a connected narrative, it was natural and almost inevitable that the wasf should be imitated. It has been noticed by many that the spontaneity and originality of the other poems disappear in these descriptions. This is due to their being written according to a stereotyped form. That the wasf was imitated when no regular marriage wasf was intended, but only a love-song, is proved by the fact that in one of the Mu'allaqât, the seven poems said to have been hung in the Caaba at Mekka in pre-Islamic times, that viz. of Amru ibn Kulthum, in Song of Solomon 4:13-16 inclusive, there is a description of a woman much in the tone of this.

Verse 1. - Behold, You are fair, my love; behold, You are fair; your eyes are as doves behind thy veil; your hair is as a flock of goats, that lie along the side of Mount Gilead. We commence, at this verse, the loving converse of the bridegroom with the bride, which we must suppose is heard as they travel together in the bridal procession.

Sexual Healing In the Confines of Marriage

The words of adoring affection are chiefly spoken by the bridegroom, as is natural in the circumstances, and the reference to the journey, and its consummation in ver. 8, make it certain that the intention is to carry us in thought to the palanquin and the breathings of first love in bridal joy. The poetry is exquisite and truly Eastern, while yet absolutely chaste and pure. The praise of the eyes is common in all erotic poetry. Her eyes gleam, in color, motion, and luster, like a pair of doves from behind the veil; showing that the bride is thought of as travelling. The bride was always deeply veiled (see Genesis 24:65), as the Roman bride wore the velum flamineum. The LXX. have mistaken the meaning, rendering, ἐκτὸς τῆς σιωπήσεώς. The veil might typify silence or reserve, but the word is tsammah, which is from a root "to veil," and is righty rendered by Symmachus κάλυμμα. The hair was long and dark, and lay down the shoulders uncovered and free, which added much to the graceful attraction of the bride. In later times it was customary for the hair to be adorned with a wreath of myrtle or roses, or a golden ornament representing Jerusalem. The goats in Syria and the neighboring countries are mostly black or dark brown, while the sheep are white. One scholar's says, "A flock of goats encamped upon a mountain (rising up, to one looking from a distance, as in a steep slope and almost perpendicularly), and as if hanging down lengthwise on its sides, presents a lovely view adorning the landscape." It would be especially lovely amid the romantic scenery of Gilead. The, verb rendered "lie along" is otherwise taken by the LXX., ἀπεκαλύφησαν, and by the Vulgate ascenderunt.

The Purpose For A Wife

The rabbis differ from one another in their renderings. One says, "which, look, down;" another, "make bare," "quit," or "descend;" another, "are seen." The modern translators vary. One says, "Shorn;" Houbigant, "hang down;" "shows itself;" Gesenius and others, "lie down;" "rolling down," "running down." A Revised Version gives, lie along, which is a very probable meaning. The reference is to the luxuriance and rich color of the hair. Gilead would be a recollection of the bride's native place.

CHAPTER III
The Purpose for Sex

God created us with the desire for sex, and we ought to understand his design that was meant for us in our relationships with others about sex. Christians absolutely need to seek God's purpose in this area of their lives. God created us male and female and because of that we will be attracted to one another, why? We are the opposite sex and it is a part of creation that woman was made for man as a part of creation. But we must learn to control our desires because having sex, and even the desire for sex with someone outside of marriage is not God's plan. God created man in his own image; in the image of God he created him; male and female he created them. God blessed them and said to them: Be Fruitful and Multiply, and Replenish the Earth (Genesis 1:26-30). God intends for a married man and woman to have sexual relations for the purpose of replenishing the earth within the confines of marriage. God wants us to have sex so we will bring forth more children into the world for him and to teach and train our children up in the wisdom of God! Had Adam and Eve decided to not have sex and have children then essentially they would have been rebelling against God's purpose and instruction. Controlling our Sex Drive, even though sex is good, it must be controlled! As we look at society we see many uncontrolled desires and sex drives running amok causing much harm and danger. People blame God for plagues and diseases but these things are caused from your own rebelliousness toward GOD! When we choose to disobey God's commands things happens because of our own foolish choices, as the bible tells us "There are ways that seems right to a man but in the end, it leads to death. Prov. 14:12.

Sexual Healing In the Confines of Marriage

Sex outside of marriage may seem so right to one but it is against the Law of GOD, you break the law you automatically start the process of punishment brought on by the hand of GOD. As with anything in life we must control it, so it will not overtake our lives and cause spiritual and emotional turmoil for us. We must control our sex drive, lest we hurt others, damage our relationships and ourselves, and sin against God. If we don't control our appetite for food we become overweight and sick. In the same way if we don't control our appetite for sex it will control us and tempt us into immoral acts of lust. That lust will lead to other things that many are not prepared to handle. More dangerous if this thing lead to danger for all parties involved. Did you know that your bodies are members of Christ himself? Shall I then take the members of Christ and unite them with a prostitute? Never! Do you know that he who unites himself with a prostitute is one with her in body? For it is said, "The two will becomes one flesh." But he who unites himself with lord is one with him in spirit. Paul uses this incident with the Corinthian church immorality ways and means to bring out GODs certification in marriage. GOD certifies a union by way of sexual relations between a man and a woman. It is the law of the land that certifies a marriage by way of documentation such as a marriage license. Does GOD recognize the law of the land? Absolutely, Paul speaks of in the book of it in Rom. 13:1, "Everyone must submit himself to the governing authorities, for there is no authority except that which God has established.

The Purpose For Sex

The authorities that exist have been established by GOD."God says that sex is a beautiful and healthy part of life when it is between a married man and woman. But he also lets us know that the sex drive must be used for his purpose Fornication is sexual intercourse between two unmarried people "the defrauding of each other". Many of us think about things with a different perspective than what many have been brought up to believe, sex without any real intention for marriage is a deception and is morally wrong. This is why God calls fornication a sin. Sex outside of the boundaries of marriage will lead the hand of GOD against you. God does not want to see us heart broken or sick from disease because we gave into sexual immorality. God loves us and wants what is best for us, to reserve having sex until we are married."For this is the will of God, that you should be sanctified: that you should avoid sexual immorality; that each of you should learn to control his own body in a way that is holy and honorable, not in passionate lust like the heathen, who do not know GOD; and that in this matter no one should wrong his brother or take advantage of him. The Lord will punish men for all such sins, as we have already told you and warned you. For GOD did not call us to be impure, but to live a holy life. (1 Thessalonians 4:3-7). Marriage is the only intended purpose for sex. Anything else perverts and distorts sexual relations and the mind, body and spirit of a person. God created sex for sexual enjoyment in marriage. The bottom line is our sex drive was created for the purpose of procreation and sexual fulfillment between a husband and a wife! Realizing the proper use of our sex drive is the first step in controlling it.

Then the Lord GOD made a woman from the rib he had taken out of the man, and he brought her to the man. Then man said, "This is now bone of my bones and flesh of my flesh; she shall be called woman, for she was taken out of man." For this reason a man will leave his father and mother and be united to his wife, and they will become one flesh. The man and his wife were both naked, and they felt no shame. (Genesis 2:23-25). The sex drive is not dirty, until we choose to abuse it. The sex drive is not sinful, until we choose to abuse it. Our sex drive is an awesome gift from God that should be used to honor and glorify God with by bringing forth children, and for our own enjoyment in marriage. The institution of marriage allows the lawful sexual union between male and female in the eyes of God and society. Since both, male and female should dedicate their lives to the Will of God and the great struggle in the journey of the meeting with God, the great struggle of the union between the two, then the pleasure derived from sex is Divinely given to enhance the union as well as to re-charge the electrical energy of the male and the female that they might continue the great journey and struggle of life. These two, properly motivated, allows the sexual union to be a life-giving experience not only in procreation and continuance of the life of the species, but, it is invigorating as well as life giving to the marriage and the struggle of these two to become as one. To look at marriage as only the legalization of the sex act is to put our minds on a level that will not bring the best out of the experience.

The Purpose For Sex

To become extreme in our view that the sex act is only for procreation and not meant by God to give pleasure to married couples is a view that is not in accord with the Will, Plan and Purpose of God. These pleasure centers in the human being, used properly and in accord with the Will of God, brings comfort, ease, consolation, rest, reward and joy to the souls that are working hard to fulfill their Divine duty and obligation.

What is the purpose of sex in marriage?
1. Procreation of human species.
2. Reward the struggle of the two to become one with the joy of the pleasure of each other's complimentary nature.
3. To give rest, relaxation and new energy to the male to continue the great mission of being producer of mastering the earth and its laws as we strives to become one who stands in the place of God at his level of development. The female in energizing the male and giving him this comfort, consolation; giving him peace and quiet of mind as a rest period between struggle is also satisfied and is pleased because she has given rest to him to work for God, her and the family. Therefore, she is rested in herself. This is the Divine Purpose of Sex in Marriage. Satan, however, has taken this natural gift of God and made mischief with it causing us to go after pleasure without struggle; without the burden or responsibility of being what God created us to be.

We have become pleasure seekers without responsibility and misusing our pleasure centers thus becoming slaves of pleasure. This has given rise to the misuse of women and the misuse of what God gave them for the man so that she becomes a prostitute – sex for hire, he becomes a pimp – using her and the need of the male for pleasure as a means of livelihood. The lust for pleasure is causing the abuse of children, male and female, and the misuse of our bodies. As a result, we are living in a morally degenerate world. We are paying the price for this moral degeneracy through the plague of AIDS and sexually transmitted diseases, which produce the destruction of the male and female and the destruction of our future. This is why we must return to God and seek to know His purpose for what He created and use everything of creation in accord with His purpose for it. Then, and only then, will we find the genuine peace, joy, and happiness that we seek. Psalms says, "Behold, how good and how pleasant it is for brethren to dwell together in unity!" Unity awards us another kind of pleasure. There is tremendous pleasure in being one with God. There is tremendous joy in knowing that we are pleasing in His sight. Let us strive for the real pleasure of life that comes from duty to God through his Son Christ Jesus; duty to ourselves; duty to our mates; duty to our families; duty to our community. Let us seek real pleasure that comes when we know that we have struggled to obey God; we have struggled to bear the burden of the great responsibility that God has placed on our shoulders; we have accepted the difficulty factor of life knowing truly that after difficulty comes ease.

CHAPTER IV
The Purpose For Marriage

What is marriage for? The answer that you'll get from children's stories is, "to live happily ever after." The answer we get from television and movies is, "to make your life miserable ever after." No two people get married in order to make themselves or each other miserable. They marry with optimism that life truly will be more meaningful and emotionally richer. Before the 1960"s, the divorce rate was a lot lower than it is today and most couples reported being fairly happy together. But then the Sexual Revolution came along and people said, "We don't need marriage anymore. Anyone can live together for however long they want to for whatever reason they want to and shouldn't have to be bound together 'till death do us part." We want freedom to express ourselves anyway we choose. We don't need God or the institution of marriage that He created." Then the minority of people who were unhappily married or who grew up in an unhappy home led the rebellion. They took over the legislatures; they took over the judicial system, they took over the entertainment industry and popular culture. They took over the schools, they have told us lie after lie in order to try to convince us that their own immoral behaviors are OK. Since this war on marriage and family began they dragged our culture down deeper and deeper into the gutter. Even though the average American's lifestyle is not like TV shows and movies make it out to be Hollywood continues to portray us that way. They are constantly pushing their immorality on us. The message is clear: If you aren't sexually promiscuous then shame on you.

In addition, Hollywood exports this false view of Americans to the rest of the world. One of the major reasons there so many enemies in the Christian, Muslim, Judaism and Asian cultures is that they think we are all a bunch of sex addicts and perverts. They don't realize that most Americans are not like that. I believe one of the gravest mistakes occurred when we lost sight of God's purposes for marriage and sex. As a result, many people see marriage and sex inside of marriage as too limiting. They say things like, "God is against sex" and "God doesn't want us to have any fun." They don't think that their needs can be met through marriage. They use various alternatives to try to meet those needs on their own. But when we gain a correct view of God's purposes for marriage, only then can we realize how God uses marriage to protect us and provide for us better than any way we can devise on our own. God tells us why He created the institution of marriage. God has at least 5 purposes for marriage and sex that are found in Genesis chapters one and two. The Trinity being first purpose for marriage and sex is to reflect God's oneness. Genesis tells us, "Then God said, 'Let us make man in our image, in our likeness.' "In order to understand oneness that two people can experience in a relationship together we need to understand God who makes that possible. To do that, we'll have to dive right in to some pretty heavy theology. You've learned somewhere that God has three persons yet is one God. Does this mean Christians can't count? Does this mean we believe in three Gods or one God?

The Purpose For Marriage

The doctrine of God's Trinity can be very confusing but once we begin to understand it we see how God experiences the ultimate oneness in relationship. In order to make any sense of this, we have to distinguish between what the one refers to and what the three refers to. The one refers to God's essence or nature, in other words, His Goodness, His Divine essence. No one else in the spiritual or physical universe has the divine essence. Indeed, there cannot be any other because there is no room for any more beings with a divine essence. God's divine essence takes up the whole universe. The divine essence cannot be divided between more than one god; otherwise it is not truly the divine essence. It is not that God is merely characterized by a divine essence; God is the divine essence and the divine essence is God. The three refers to three distinct persons. All the persons of the triune God share the divine essence. There is only one divine essence, but there are three persons who share this same nature. The members of the trinity are distinct (The Father, the Son and the Holy Spirit). Does it sound like I just contradicted myself? I haven't because the difference is this. The gods of mythology are distinct beings that act independently. They each have their own agenda. They are seen scheming against and fighting with each other. In 180 degree contrast, the members of the trinity are perfectly and deeply interrelated. They have an unbreakable unity. It is said, "For in the divine life there is no isolation, no insulation, no secretiveness, and no fear of being transparent to another."

Sexual Healing In the Confines of Marriage

So while each of the divine persons (Father, Son, and Holy Spirit) fully similarly...We cannot remove one person from this intimate relationship and have the other two remain intact....Because the members of the Trinity share the same essence and mutually indwell one another, they also act as one rather than in isolation from one another. Even though three distinct wills exist within the Trinity, only one will is ultimately expressed, which indicates the deep unity of the Godhead. So we could answer the question, What is God like? By saying, "a triangle," but a triangle isn't personal. Instead, God answers the question with, "I am giving you a marriage relationship not just to know intellectually what I am like but to experience what I am like." What a teacher! In a marriage relationship we can experience the wonder and beauty of being two distinct individuals with two distinct wills being united by sharing the essence of humanness. God wants the marriage relationship to be the earthly, visible, tangible model for this ultimate oneness. God made mankind in such a way that males and females are distinctly different. So when a man and a woman come together they are two distinctly different people with not only personality differences but gender differences as well. When these two distinctly different genders are brought together they begin to reflect God's oneness. Genesis 1:26 - 28 tells us, "Then God said, 'Let us (the triune God) make man in our image, in our likeness...' So God created man in his own image, in the image of God he created him; male and female he created them."An individual, while made in the image of God, can not reflect God's oneness.

The Purpose For Marriage

A man and a man or a woman and a woman can not reflect God's oneness. Homosexuality can not reflect God's oneness. Instead, it is a counterfeit because to reflect God's oneness requires a male and a female. Why settle for less than the real thing? We'll talk more about homosexuality later in the next book "Save the Family." Now how does this oneness in relationship protect and provide for us? We are emotional and social creatures. We are made to love and to be loved. We are made for oneness with another person. But this oneness can't happen in one night. It takes a commitment to be loyal and faithful to only one person. This commitment is called marriage. This oneness doesn't even happen completely on a honeymoon. It takes years of getting to know each other, working together, living together, fighting together, relating together to experience the true depth of that deep oneness that is possible. So through marriage our needs for deep intimacy and emotional connectedness are met better than any other way. I'd better say something brief about celibacy here so I'm not misunderstood. Celibacy is a God-given exception. It is a calling and a choice. Because God calls a person to celibacy He will take care of that person's needs for deep intimacy and emotional connectedness through His relationship with that person. Moving on, tragically, many young people mistakenly assume that just because their parents don't share emotional intimacy then no one, including them, can find it in marriage. It doesn't have to be that way.

Sexual Healing In the Confines of Marriage

A man and a woman can go through ups and downs but through it all one can come to experience a deep emotional intimacy beyond what one ever thought was possible as one moves toward being married. To achieve oneness on our own without God whether inside or outside of marriage, we rob ourselves of what we are made for. God designed marriage to protect us and provide for us. In Genesis we read, "God blessed them and said to them, Be fruitful and increase in number; fill the earth." The second purpose for marriage and sex is to procreate, that is to make babies and thereby keep mankind from becoming extinct. The first purpose is to be productive in the world, plant some seeds that they grow to make an impact in the world. Over the years, a married couple has sex far more often than for the purpose of producing children. If sex was only for procreation, God had to make it enjoyable so that we would want to do it more often than just for children. Procreation multiplies a godly heritage. Part of God's strategic plan is that through this lineage of godly descendants, Satan's evil rebellion would be defeated. You see, according to various passages in the Bible we learn that before the physical universe was created, God created the angels, including Lucifer, whose name meant "bearer of light," "Morning Star" He was the most awesome angel there was. He got conceited and led a third of all the angels in a coup attempt to replace God as the ultimate ruler of the universe. If he had really understood God he wouldn't have tried such a foolish and futile act. Instead of locking them up in prison or wiping them out of their very existence, God formulated a plan.

The Purpose For Marriage

Remember, Lucifer, who is now called Satan, meaning the adversary or opponent, isn't like God. He doesn't know the future and can't figure out God's plan. He may not know anymore about God's plan than we know, and that's reassuring. Anyway, part of God's strategy for dealing with this rebellion was to create the physical universe and planet earth and particularly mankind. God simply hasn't given us enough information to completely understand how this is important to His strategy but He isn't obligated to inform us or Satan of His battle plans. One thing is for sure, Satan hates God and anything that reminds him of God. It just so happened that God created mankind in his image, that is, to be finite replicas of the infinite God. So every time a new human being is conceived in its mother's womb there is another replica of God. So God told us to fill the earth with images of Him. Can you imagine anything else that would drive Satan crazier than to turn every corner and see a reminder of the very God he hates? God made humans to be uniquely different than all other living things. Angels cannot reproduce and make more angels. And while sexual reproduction is important to all living creatures it is given a cosmic significance when it comes to human reproduction. When humans have sex to make babies it takes on the most mysterious meaning of making other humans that bear God's image. This is why abortion is wrong. It treats a human baby like the flesh of any other animal when instead it is a person that bears God's image. It delights Satan when babies are killed because then he doesn't have to risk the possibly of them growing up to become Christians and joining the fight against him.

Sexual Healing In the Confines of Marriage

There is yet another reason God gave us sex and that is, to teach us to give unselfishly to one another. God endowed men and women with certain anatomical parts that produce pleasure but are not necessary for intercourse and procreation. Humans have the ability to prolong sex and to give and receive mutual pleasure. We can express love and affection by giving pleasure to our mate that goes way beyond what is necessary to simply make babies. Both marriage partners enjoy sex more when they learn to give and receive this extra pleasure. Their relationship is enriched and deepened as they learn to give to each other. Genesis 1:26 tells us, God blessed them and said to them, "Be fruitful and increase in number; fill the earth and subdue it. Rule over the fish of the sea and the birds of the air and over every living creature that moves on the ground."Lions are not the king of the beasts, humans are. Even though God built many self-managing checks and balances into nature He put mankind in charge of nature. Instead of managing His creation Himself, God chose to delegate the task to mankind. What a responsibility! In chapter 2 of Genesis we learn that man was created to be a steward of the land. Even before Adam sinned God put him in the Garden of Eden "to work it and take care of it." (Gen. 2:15) As wonderful as the description of the Garden sounds it was not self-maintaining. This shows us that work is not the result of Adam's sin. The part of the curse involving work seems to deal with the frustration we feel when we work.

The Purpose For Marriage

Work is something God created us to do in order to manage His creation. Now, once we understand how special God's creation is and what kind of responsibility we have to be good managers of it, we realize we must work together effectively and constantly depend on God for wisdom and strength. The family unit is uniquely designed to manage God's creation. When we are working together as a family unit we experience God's protection against the hostilities of nature and He provides us with the food and resources we need to live. Inevitably, the picture that comes to mind is a farming family. The husband is out plowing the fields and doing manly work. The wife is cooking, cleaning, canning fruits and vegetables, knitting clothes and doing things for the children. She's doing the "woman's work."But most of us don't live on a farm. So how are we to apply this business of managing God's creation together if we don't deal directly with the land? There are more gender differences than just physical strength. And the gender differences run so much deeper than merely who has to do the cooking and cleaning and take out the trash. Males and females think differently, approach problems differently, feel differently, etc. Paul says" For the husband is the head of the wife as Christ is the head of the church, his body, of which he is our Savior. Now as the church submits to Christ, so also wives should submit to their husbands in everything.""Husbands, love your wives, just as Christ loved the church and gave himself up for her to make her holy, cleansing her by the washing with water through the word, and to present her to himself as a radiant church, without stain or wrinkle or any other blemish, but holy and blameless.

In this same way, husbands ought to love their wives as their own bodies. He who loves his wife loves himself. After all, no one ever hated his own body, but he feeds and cares for it, just as Christ does the church for we are members of his body. For this reason a man will leave his father and mother and be united to his wife, and the two will become one flesh. This is a profound mystery, but I am talking about Christ and the church. However, each one of you also must love his wife as he loves himself, and the wife must respect her husband."When a husband loves his wife with the selfless, unconditional, sacrificial and trustworthy love with which Christ loves us and the church, his wife normally should have no problem at all submitting to him. If she can't, she needs to examine her own self to find out why. Finally, it is the husband's mission in their marriage to lead her to more spiritual maturity so that she reflects God's character more and more beautifully. So the marriage relationship is to serve as a model of the church's relationship with Christ, while the church's relationship with Christ serves as a model for the marriage relationship. This is truly an amazing, beautiful thing and an incredibly powerful weapon against Satan and his rebellious forces.

CHAPTER V
The Song of Solomon

Song of Solomon 1:1 contains the title of the book: literally, A song of the songs (Heb., Shîr hashîrîm), which to Solomon, i.e., of which Solomon is author. This has been understood as meaning "one of Solomon's songs," with allusion to the 1,005 songs (1Kings 4:32) which that monarch composed. But when in Hebrew a compound idea is to be expressed definitely, the article is prefixed to the word in the genitive. So here not merely "a song of songs" (comp. holy of holies), i.e., "a very excellent song," but "The song of songs," i.e., the most excellent or surpassing song. For the question of authorship and date of poem, see Excursus I. Song of Solomon 1:1. The Song of Songs — The most excellent of all songs. And so this might well be called, whether we consider the author of it, who was a great prince, and the wisest of all mortal men; or the subject of it, which is not Solomon, but a greater than Solomon, even Christ, and his marriage with the church; or the matter of it, which is most lofty, containing in it the noblest of all the mysteries contained either in the Old or the New Testament; most pious and pathetical, breathing forth the hottest flames of love between Christ and his people, most sweet and comfortable, and useful to all that read it with serious and Christian eyes. 1:1 This is the Song of songs, excellent above any others, for it is wholly taken up with describing the excellences of Christ, and the love between him and his redeemed people. The "Song of Songs," the best or most excellent of songs.

Which is Solomon's - literally, "to" or "for Solomon," i. e., belonging to Solomon as its author or concerning him as its subject. In a title or inscription, the former interpretation is to be preferred. A single emblem is a type; the actual rites, incidents, and persons of the Old Testament were appointed types of truths afterwards to be revealed. But the allegory is a continued metaphor, in which the circumstances are palpably often purely imagery, while the thing signified is altogether real. The clue to the meaning of the Song is not to be looked for in the allegory itself, but in other parts of Scripture. "It lies in the casket of revelation an exquisite gem, engraved with emblematical characters, with nothing literal thereon to break the consistency of their beauty". This accounts for the name of God not occurring in it. Whereas in the parable the writer narrates, in the allegory he never does so. The Song throughout consists of immediate addresses either of Christ to the soul, or of the soul to Christ. "The experimental knowledge of Christ's loveliness and the believer's love is the best commentary on the whole of this allegorical Song". Like the curiously wrought Oriental lamps, which do not reveal the beauty of their transparent emblems until lighted up within, so the types and allegories of Scripture, "the lantern to our path" [Ps 119:105], need the inner light of the Holy Spirit of Jesus to reveal their significance. The details of the allegory are not to be too minutely pressed.

The Song of Solomon

In the Song, with an Oriental profusion of imagery, numbers of lovely, sensible objects are aggregated not strictly congruous, but portraying jointly by their very diversity the thousand various and seemingly opposite beauties which meet together in Christ. The unity of subject throughout, and the recurrence of the same expressions (So 2:6, 7; 3:5; 8:3, 4; 2:16; 6:3; 7:10; 3:6; 6:10; 8:5), prove the unity of the poem, in opposition to those who make it consist of a number of separate erotic songs. The sudden transitions (for example, from the midnight knocking at a humble cottage to a glorious description of the King) accord with the alternations in the believer's experience. However various the divisions assigned be, most have observed four breaks (whatever more they have imagined), followed by four abrupt beginnings (So 2:7; 3:5; 5:1; 8:4). Thus there result five parts, all alike ending in full repose and refreshment. We read (1Ki 4:32) that Solomon's songs were "a thousand and five." The odd number five added over the complete thousand makes it not unlikely that the "five" refers to the Song of songs, consisting of five parts. It answers to the idyllic poetry of other nations. The Jews explain it of the union of Jehovah and ancient Israel; the allusions to the temple and the wilderness accord with this; some Christians of Christ and the Church; others of Christ and the individual believer. All these are true; for the Church is one in all ages, the ancient typifying the modern Church, and its history answering to that of each individual soul in it. Jesus "sees all, as if that all were one, loves one, as if that one we're all."

"The time suited the manner of this revelation; because types and allegories belonged to the old dispensation, which reached its ripeness under Solomon, when the temple was built". "The daughter of Zion at that time was openly married to Jehovah"; for it is thenceforth that the prophets, in reproving Israel's subsequent sin, speak of it as a breach of her marriage covenant. The songs heretofore sung by her were the preparatory hymns of her childhood; "the last and crowning 'Song of Songs' was prepared for the now mature maiden against the day of her marriage to the King of kings" [Origen]. Solomon was peculiarly fitted to clothe this holy mystery with the lovely natural imagery with which the Song abounds; for "he spoke of trees, from the cedar in Lebanon, even unto the hyssop that springs out of the wall" (1Ki 4:33). A higher qualification was his knowledge of the eternal Wisdom or Word of God (Pr 8:1-36), the heavenly bridegroom. David, his father, had prepared the way, in Psalms 45 and 72; the son perfected the allegory. It seems to have been written in early life, long before his declension; for after it a song of holy gladness would hardly be appropriate. It was the song of his first love, in the kindness of his youthful espousals to Jehovah. Like other inspired books, its sense is not to be restricted to that local and temporary one in which the writer may have understood it; it extends to all ages, and shadows forth everlasting truth (1Pe 1:11, 12; 2Pe 1:20, 21). "Oh that I knew how all thy lights combine, and the configurations of their glory, Seeing not only how each verse doth shine, but all the constellations of the story."—Herbert.

The Song of Solomon

Three notes of time occur: (1) The Jewish Church speaks of the Gentile Church (So 8:8) towards the end; (2) Christ speaks to the apostles (So 5:1) in the middle; (3) The Church speaks of the coming of Christ (So 1:2) at the beginning. Thus we have, in direct order, Christ about to come, and the cry for the advent; Christ finishing His work on earth, and the last supper; Christ ascended, and the call of the Gentiles. In another aspect we have: (1) In the individual soul the longing for the manifestation of Christ to it, and the various alternations in its experience (So 1:2, 4; 2:8; 3:1, 4, 6, 7) of His manifestation; (2) The abundant enjoyment of His sensible consolations, which is soon withdrawn through the bride's carelessness (So 5:1-3, &c.), and her longings after Him, and reconciliation (So 5:8-16; 6:3, &c.; So 7:1, &c.); (3) Effects of Christ's manifestation on the believer; namely, assurance, labors of love, anxiety for the salvation of the impenitent, eagerness for the Lord's second coming (So 7:10, 12; 8:8-10, 14). So 1:1-17. Canticle I.—(So 1:2-2:7)—The Bride Searching for and Finding the King. The song of songs—The most excellent of all songs, Hebrew idiom (Ex 29:37; De 10:14). A foretaste on earth of the "new song" to be sung in glory (Re 5:9; 14:3; 15:2-4). Solomon's—"King of Israel," or "Jerusalem," is not added, as in the opening of Proverbs and Ecclesiastes, not because Solomon had not yet ascended the throne, but because his personality is hid under that of Christ, the true Solomon (equivalent to Prince of Peace). The earthly Solomon is not introduced, which would break the consistency of the allegory. Though the bride bears the chief part, the Song throughout is not hers, but that of her "Solomon." He animates her. He and she, the Head and the members, form but one Christ. Aaron prefigured Him as priest; Moses, as prophet; David, as a suffering king; Solomon, as the triumphant prince of peace. The camp in the wilderness represents the Church in the world; the peaceful reign of Solomon, after all enemies had been subdued, represents the Church in heaven, of which joy the Song gives a foretaste. A description of the earnest longing of the church after Christ, Son 1:1-4. A confession of her deformity; prayed for direction. Son 1:5-7. Christ's direction and command, Son 1:8. He showed his love to her both for her strength and comeliness, Son 1:9,10, and gives her gracious promises, Son 1:11. The church's commendation of Christ both for the sweetness of fellowship with him, and the excellence of ordinances, Son 1:12-17. The Song of Songs, most excellent of all songs, whether composed by profane or sacred authors, by Solomon and/or by any other. So this Hebrew phrase is understood in other cases, as the holy of holies signifies the most holy; and the highest King is called King of kings; and there are multitudes of such instances, as hath been oft observed. And so this might well be called, whether you consider the author of it, who was a great prince, and the wisest of all mortal men, the two Adams only excepted; or the subject of it, which is not Solomon,

The Song of Solomon

but a greater than Solomon, even Christ, and his marriage with the church, as hath been noted; or the matter of it, which is most lofty and mysterious, containing in it the greatest and noblest of all the mysteries contained either in the Old or the New Testament; most pious and pathetical, breathing forth the hottest flames of love between Christ and his people; most sweet, and comfortable, and useful to all that read it with serious and Christian eyes. Nor is it the worse because profane and wanton wits abuse it, and endeavor to fasten their absurd and filthy senses upon some passages in it. The truth is, this book requires a sober and pious, not a lascivious and foolish readier; for which reason some of the ancient Hebrews advised young men to forbear the reading of it, till they were thirty years old. Which is Solomon's; which was composed by Solomon; but whether before his fall, or after his repentance, is not easy to determine, nor necessity to be known. The Song of songs, which is Solomon's. Wrote by Solomon, king of Israel, as the "amanuensis" of the Holy Ghost; and not by Hezekiah and his men, as the Jews say (k): or, "concerning Solomon" (l); Christ, of whom Solomon was a type; see Sol 3:7; of his person, excellencies, love to his church, care of her, and concern for her; and of the nearness and communion he admitted her to, and indulged her with the Jews have a saying (m), that wherever the word Solomon is used in this song, the Holy One is meant, the holy God, or Messiah: it is called "the Song of songs", because the most excellent, as the Holy of holies, King of kings.

which, with the Hebrews, express a superlative; this being more excellent than the one hundred and five songs, written by Solomon, or than any human composure whatever; yea, preferable to all Scriptural songs, as to subject, manner of style, and copiousness of it. 1) The rose.—Heb., chabatseleth. The identification of this flower is a much vexed question. From its derivation, it should be a bulbous plant (batsal—a bulb), and it happens that the flower which for other reasons best satisfies the requirements is of this kind, viz., the Sweet-scented Narcissus (Narcissus tazetta). "Others have suggested the crocus, of which there are many species very common, but they are deficient in perfume, and there is no bulb more fragrant than the narcissus; it is, besides, one of which the Orientals arc passionately fond. While it is in flower it is to be seen in all the bazaars, and the men as well as the women always carry two or three blossoms, at which they are continually smelling" (Tristram, Nat. Hist.) Song of Solomon 2:1-2. I am the rose of Sharon — These are the words of the bridegroom. He compares himself to the rose and lily, for fragrancy and beauty. Sharon was a very fruitful place, and famous for roses. As the lily among thorns — Compared with thorns, which it unspeakably exceeds in glory and beauty; so is my love — So far doth my church, or people, excel all other assemblies. The title of daughter is often given to whole nations. These are Christ's words, to which the spouse makes the following reply. 2:1-7 Believers are beautiful, as clothed in the righteousness of Christ; and fragrant, as adorned with the graces of his Spirit; and they thrive under the refreshing beams of the Sun of righteousness.

The Song of Solomon

The lily is a very noble plant in the East; it grows to a considerable height, but has a weak stem. The church is weak in herself, yet is strong in Him that supports her. The wicked, the daughters of this world, who have no love to Christ, are as thorns, worthless and useless, noxious and hurtful. Corruptions are thorns in the flesh; but the lily now among thorns, shall be transplanted into that paradise where there is no brier or thorn. The world is a barren tree to the soul; but Christ is a fruitful one. And when poor souls are parched with convictions of sin, with the terrors of the law, or the troubles of this world, weary and heavy laden, they may find rest in Christ. It is not enough to pass by this shadow, but we must sit down under it. Believers have tasted that the Lord Jesus is gracious; his fruits are all the precious privileges of the new covenant, purchased by his blood, and communicated by his Spirit; promises are sweet to a believer, and precepts also. Pardons are sweet, and peace of conscience sweet. If our mouths are out of taste for the pleasures of sin, Divine consolations will be sweet to us. Christ brings the soul to seek and to find comforts through his ordinances, which are as a banqueting-house where his saints feast with him. The love of Christ, manifested by his death, and by his word, is the banner he displays, and believers resort to it. How much better is it with the soul when sick from love to Christ, than when surfeited with the love of this world! And though Christ seemed to have withdrawn, yet he was even then a very present help. All his saints are in his hand, which tenderly holds their aching heads.

Sexual Healing In the Confines of Marriage

Finding Christ thus nigh to her, the soul is in great care that her communion with him is not interrupted. We easily grieve the Spirit by wrong tempers. Let those who have comfort, fear sinning it away. The division of the chapters is unfortunate; Cant. 2 ought to have begun at Sol 1:15, or Cant. 1 to have been continued to Sol 2:7. The bride replies, "And I am like a lovely wild flower springing at the root of the stately forest-trees." The majority of Christian fathers assigned this verse to the King (Christ). Hebrew commentators generally assign it to the bride. It is quite uncertain what flower is meant by the word rendered (here and Isaiah 35:1) "rose." The etymology is in favor of its being a bulbous plant (the white narcissus). "Sharon" is usually the proper name of the celebrated plain from Joppa to Caesarea, between the hill-country and the sea, and travelers have remarked the abundance of flowers with which this plain is still carpeted in spring. But in the time of Eusebius and Jerome there was a smaller plain of Sharon (Saron) situated between Mount Tabor and the sea of Tiberias, which would be very near the bride's native home if that were Shunem. So 2:1-17. 1. rose—if applied to Jesus Christ, it, with the white lily (lowly, 2Co 8:9), answers to "white and ruddy" (So 5:10). But it is rather the meadow-saffron: the Hebrew means radically a plant with a pungent bulb, inapplicable to the rose. So Syriac, it is of a white and violet color. The bride thus speaks of herself as lowly though lovely, in contrast with the lordly "apple" or citron tree, the bridegroom (So 2:3); so the "lily" is applied to her (So 2:2), Sharon—(Isa 35:1, 2).

The Song of Solomon

In North Palestine, between Mount Tabor and Lake Tiberias (1Ch 5:16). Septuagint and Vulgate translate it, "a plain"; though they err in this, the Hebrew Bible not elsewhere favoring it, yet the parallelism to valleys shows that, in the proper name Sharon, there is here a tacit reference to its meaning of lowliness. Beauty, delicacy, and lowliness, are to be in her, as they were in Him (Mt 11:29).The excellency of the majesty of Christ, Song of Solomon 2:1, and of his church, Song of Solomon 2:2. The benefits which the church receives from him, Song of Solomon 2:3. Christ's love to his church, Song of Solomon 2:4. The church sick of love; her prayer for help, Song of Solomon 2:5. His ears for her in this condition, Song of Solomon 2:6. The hope and calling of the church, Song of Solomon 2:10-13. Christ's care of the church, Song of Solomon 2:14,15. The profession of the church; her faith and hope, Song of Solomon 2:16,17. These are the words either, Of the spouse, continuing her discourse. Or rather, Of the bridegroom, drawing forth the church's affections to him. He compares himself to the rose and lily, for fragrance and beauty. Nor is it in the least degree indecent that Christ should thus commend himself, partly because his Excellency is so transcendently great, that he is free from all suspicion of vanity and self-flattery; and partly because it is suitable to the style of such writings, and to the present design of recommending himself to the affection of his spouse. He mentions the rose of Sharon, which was a very fruitful place, as is evident from 1 Chronicles 27:29 Isaiah 33:9 65:10, and famous for roses, as may seem probable from Isaiah 35:1,2. Or, as others translate it, the rose of the field, which may note that Christ is not only pleasant and beautiful, but free and communicative, offering himself to all that come to him. The lily is a beautiful and glorious creature, Matthew 6:29, especially to one who beholds it through a magnifying glass. He said, the lily of the valleys, because they grew and flourished best in such low and waterish grounds. I am the rose of Sharon, and the lily of the valleys. Whether Christ, or the church, is here speaking, is not certain: most of the Jewish writers, and some Christian interpreters, take them to be the words of the church, expressing the excellency of her grace, loveliness, and beauty, she had from Christ; and intimating also her being in the open fields, exposed to many dangers and enemies, and so needed his protection. The church may be compared to a "rose", for its beautiful color and sweet odor, and for its delight in sunny places, where it thrives best, and is most fragrant. This figure is exceeding just; not only the beauty of women is expressed by the color of the rose, as is common in poems of this kind; to give instances of it would be endless; some have had the name of Rhoda from hence; see Acts 12:13. No rose can be more beautiful in color, and delightful to the eye, than the church is in the eyes of Christ, as clothed with his righteousness, and adorned with the graces of his Spirit: nor is any rose of a more sweet and fragrant smell than the persons of believers are to God and Christ, being considered in him; and even their graces, when in exercise, yea, their duties and services, when performed in faith; and, as the rose, they grow and thrive under the warming, comforting, and refreshing beams of the sun of righteousness, where they delight to be. The church may also be compared to a "lily of the valleys", as she is, in the next verse, to one among thorns.

The Song of Solomon

This is a very beautiful flower next in nobleness to the rose; its whiteness is singularly excellent; no plant more fruitful, and no flower exceeds it in height; in some countries, it rises up three cubits high; has a weak neck or body, insufficient to bear the weight of its head. The church may be compared to a lily, for her beauty and fragrance, as to a rose; and the redness of the rose, and the whiteness of the lily, meeting in her, make her somewhat like her beloved, white and ruddy; like the lily, being arrayed in fine linen, clean and white, the righteousness of the saints; and like it for fruitfulness, as it is in good works, under the influence of divine grace, and grows up on high into her head, Christ Jesus; and though weak in herself, yet strong in him, who supports her, and not she him: and the church may be compared to a "lily of the valleys"; which may not describe any particular lily, and what we now call so; but only expresses the place where it grows, in low places, where plants are in danger of being plucked and trodden upon; though they may have more moisture and verdure than those in higher places; so the church of Christ is sometimes in a low estate, exposed to enemies, and liable to be trampled and trodden under foot by them, and to be carried away with the flood of persecution, were it not guarded by divine power; and, being watered with the dews of grace, it becomes flourishing and fruitful. But the more commonly received opinion is, that these are the words of Christ concerning himself; and which indeed best become him, and are more agreeable to his style and language, John 14:6; and suit best with the words in the Sol 2:2, as one observes (a); nor is it unfit taken by the bridegroom to himself, since it is sometimes given by lovers to men (b). Christ may be compared to a rose for its color and smell; to the rose for its red color: and which may be expressive of the truth of his humanity, and of his bloody sufferings in it; and this, with the whiteness of the lily, finishes the description of him for his beauty, Sol 5:10; and for its sweet smell; which denotes the same things for which he is before compared to spikenard, myrrh, and campfire. The rose, as Pliny says (c), delights not in fat soils and rich clays, but in rubbish, and roses that grow there are of the sweetest smell; and such was the earth about Sharon (d); and to a rose there Christ is compared, to show the excellency and preferableness of him to all others. The word is only used here and in Isaiah 35:1. Where it is in many versions rendered a "lily": it seems to be compounded of two words; one which signifies to "cover" and hide, and another which signifies a "shadow"; and so may be rendered, "the covering shadow": but for what reason a rose should be so called is not easy to say; unless it can be thought to have the figure of an umbrella; or that the rose tree in those parts was so large, as to be remarkable for its shadow; like that Montfaucon (e) saw, in a garden at Ravenna, under the shadow of the branches of which more than forty men could stand: Christ is sometimes compared to trees for their shadow, which is pleasant and reviving, as in Sol 2:3. Some render it, "the flower of the field" (f); which may be expressive of the meanness of Christ in the eyes of men; of his not being of human production; of his being accessible; and of his being liable to be trampled upon, as he has been. And as he is compared to a rose, so to a "lily", for its color, height, and fruitfulness; expressive of his purity in

The Song of Solomon

himself, of his superiority to angels and men, and of his being filled with the fruits and blessings of grace; and to a lily of the valleys, denoting his wonderful condescension in his low estate of humiliation, and his delight in dwelling with the humble and lowly: some render the words, "I am the rose of Sharon, with the lily of the valleys" (g); by the former epithet meaning himself; and by the latter his church, his companion, in strict union and communion with him; of whom the following words are spoken. 1. By night] Lit. In the nights. In Psalm 16:7 the same phrase is translated "in the night seasons," and some understand it here of the night hours. But in none of the few passages in which the plural lçlôth occurs, is it used in this sense. In all it refers to more nights than one, not to the several parts of one night. It would therefore seem that she means to say, that one night after another she dreamt that she missed and sought her lover. More than once that had come to her, so that more than one night must have passed before she told the dream.[on my bed] This means that the dream came to her when she was in her bed. The repetition of I sought expresses well the continued and repeated searching always ending in failure, which is so characteristic of dreams and so painful. The place where she first looked for him is left indeterminate as it often is in dreams. Song of Solomon 3:1-5. A Dream almost all commentators agree that we have here a dream narrated to some persons, in which the Shulammite seems to herself to have sought her lover in the city and failed to find him. to return at sunset.

Those who take the dramatic view think of it as narrated to the women of the court. One may view it that the Shulammite expected her lover He did not come, and so her agitated heart sought him in this dream, which she tells to her companions, adding the refrain already used in Song of Solomon 2:7, which deprecates the stirring up of love before it arises spontaneously. Some regards to the end of ch. 2 as dealing only with a waking dream, and not a real incident, thinks of this as a narrative of what she remembered to have dreamed during her sad night in the king's palace. Some again, may think of the lover as Solomon, considers the dream to be one that came to her night after night, when she had become doubtful of the king's love for her. Others view is one that entirely contradicts this theory that lovers could not meet and have such intercourse as is depicted in the book before marriage. He makes this a strong point in his criticism of the dramatic theory, yet here he says of this section, "The bride speaks. She narrates a dream she had as a girl, for what she narrates can be understood only as a dream. She had so loved her husband for a length of time that she dreamt she was married to him." Most, because of a misunderstanding of the passage and on other insufficient grounds, would strike out the verses altogether. In any case they describe a dream, and of all the suggestions as to the occasion there is one that seems the best. Verse 1. - By night on my bed I sought him whom my soul loves: I sought him, but I found him not. The bride is probably relating a dream. The time referred to is the close of the day on which she had been visited by her lover. She is retired to rest, and dreams that she searches for the beloved object in the neighboring city (cf. Job 33:15).

The Song of Solomon

It is another way of telling her love. She is always longing for the beloved one. She had been waiting for him, and he came not, and retired to rest with a heart troubled and anxious because her lover did not appear as she expected at the evening hour. The meaning may be "night after night" (Song of Solomon 3:8), or the plural maybe used poetically for the singular. It's observed that "by night on my bed" is opposed to midday couch (2 Samuel 4:5), merely to express what came into her thoughts at night in her dreams or as the result of a dream. It is difficult to avoid the conclusion that the bride intends to represent herself as suffering from self-reproach in having grieved her lover and kept him away from her. In that case the typical meaning would be simple and direct. The soul grieves when it is conscious of estrangement from him whom it loves, and the sense of separation becomes intolerable, impelling to new efforts to deepen the spiritual life. A Biblical Commentary on the Old Testament

11 For, lo! the winter is past,

The rain is over, is gone.

12 The flowers appear in the land;

The time of song has come,

And the voice of the turtle makes itself heard in our land.

13 The fig-tree spices her green figs,

And the vines stand in bloom, they diffuse fragrance; - Rise up, my love, my fair one, and go forth! The Song of Solomon is regarded today as probably one of the most obscure and difficult books in the Bible. But it may surprise you to know that throughout the Christian centuries it has been one of the most read and most loved books of all. During the dark days before the Protestant Reformation when the Albaneses fled the Catholic church and John Huss led his small bands of Christians up into Bohemia, this was one of the books of the Bible that was frequently read, quoted, referred to and memorized. It was a great comfort to them. In the days after the Reformation. in the time of the bitter persecution of the Covenanters of Scotland, out of which came the Presbyterian Church under the leadership of John Knox and others, this again was one of the most frequently read and most often quoted books. It brought the Covenanters great comfort and sustained the spirits of those men and women who were hunted like animals throughout the mountains and glens of Europe. This is the last of the five books of the Old Testament. Job is the first, then Psalms. Proverbs, Ecclesiastes, and last. the Song of Solomon. Each of these books reveals one of the basic elements of man. Job is the voice of the spirit, the deepest part of man's nature, which is why the book of Job is perennially a puzzle to us. In the words of one of the Psalms, it is one of those books in which "deep called to deep;" you can't read it without recognizing its profundities. It is almost impossible to exhaust them. Here is the voice of man crying out through pain and struggle for God. Job says, "Oh, that I knew where I might find him." (Job 23:3) The books of Psalms, Proverbs, and Ecclesiastes form a

The Song of Solomon

trilogy which sets forth the voice of the soul. The soul of man is made up of three parts: mind, emotion and will; and in these books you have the expression of these elements in man's character. Psalms is the book of the heart, of the emotions, and in it you will find reflected every emotion known to man. This is the book to turn to whenever emotion is strong in your life to find an answering psalm that will reflect and meet your mood. That is why the Psalms have always been such loved portions of scripture. The book of Ecclesiastes is the voice or expression of the mind of man. It is a penetrating inquiry into life, searching after answers, and in that book all the philosophies that man has ever discovered find their expression. Ecclesiastes speaks of man searching for answers. And the answer it comes up with, because it approaches life only on the level of the intellect, is that all is vanity and emptiness; futility is stamped upon all things. That is what the mind discovers without Christ. The book of Proverbs is the expression of the will in man, summed up in the most quoted of the proverbs, "Trust in the Lord with all your heart, and do not rely on your own insight. In all your ways acknowledge him [that is the choice of the will], and he will make straight your paths." (Prov. 3:5-6) The mind and the heart together must apply knowledge to the direction of the will to choose the right way. All through Proverbs you will find the emphasis is on the appeal to the will. Now if the book of Job is the cry of the spirit, and Psalms, Proverbs and Ecclesiastes the cry of the soul, the Song of Solomon is preeminently the cry of the body in its essential yearning. And what is the essential yearning of the body? For love.

Sexual Healing In the Confines of Marriage

Therefore, the theme of this book is love. It is an eastern love song, an oriental love poem, and there is no use denying that. It is frankly and fully that. It is a revelation of all that was intended in the divinely given function that we call sex. It is sex as God intended sex to be, involving not just a physical activity, but the whole nature of man. For sex permeates our lives; many scholars was right about that. But sexual response and impulse touches us more than physically. It also touches us emotionally, and even spiritually; God made us that way. There is nothing wrong with this. But this is where Victorianism went astray. It was pushed to extremism by the enemy. (This is always the devil's activity---to push attitudes toward sex into extreme positions.) So sex went into prudishness, as though it were some unmentionable subject, as though it were something that should be kept locked up in drawers and hidden away behind curtains. But that is not the way you find it in the Bible. In the Bible, sex, like every other subject, is handled frankly and dealt with forthrightly. It is set forth as God intended it to be. So first and foremost, the Song of Solomon is a love song describing with frankness and yet with purity the delight of a man and his wife in one another's bodies. There is nothing pornographic or obscene about it, nothing licentious. As you read though it, you can see how beautifully and chastely it approaches this subject. The book comes to us in what we would call musical play form. The characters in this play are Solomon, the young king of Israel---this was written in the beginning of his reign, in all the beauty and manliness of his youth---and the Shulammite. She was a simple country last of unusual loveliness who fell in love with the king when he was disguised as

The Song of Solomon

a shepherd lad working in one of his own vineyards in the north of Israel. In the book of Ecclesiastes, Solomon tells us that he undertook expeditions to discover what life was like on various levels. Once he disguised himself as a simple country shepherd lad, and in that state he had met this young lady. They fell in love, and after they had promised themselves to each other, he went away and was gone for some time. The Shulammite girl cries out for him in her loneliness. Then comes the announcement that the king in all his glory is coming to visit the valley. While the girl is interested in this, she is not really concerned because her heart longs for her lover. But suddenly she receives word that the king wants to see her. She doesn't know why until she goes to see him, and discovers that he is her shepherd lad. He takes her away and they are married in the palace. The play is set in Jerusalem, the capital of Israel, and a chorus of singers, referred to as the daughters of Jerusalem, asks certain leading questions from time to time during the account of the events leading up to the courtship, bethrothal and marriage. The Shulammite girl addresses them on three occasions. It is interesting to note that the word "Shulammite" is the feminine form of Solomon. Therefore we would call this lady Mrs. Solomon. She is the bride, and we read of her encounter with this young man their courtship and the strength and the methods and the delights of love. The language of the book is highly poetical and figurative and there may also be some difficulty determining who is speaking at any one time.

But you can distinguish the different speakers in this way: the bridegroom always refers to her as "my love," and the bride calls him "my beloved." And as each describes the other you can see the passion and the rapture of love. Here is the language of love as she describes him: My beloved is all radiant and ruddy, distinguished among ten thousand. His head is the finest gold; his locks are wavy, black as a raven. His eyes are like doves beside springs of water, bathed in milk, fitly set. His cheeks are like beds of spices yielding fragrance. His lips are lilies, distilling liquid myrrh. His arms are rounded gold, set with jewels. His body is ivory work, encrusted with sapphires. His legs are alabaster columns, set upon bases of gold. His appearance is like Lebanon, choice as the cedars. His speech is most sweet, and he is altogether desirable. This is my beloved and this is my friend, O daughters of Jerusalem. (Sol. 5:10-16)

And he describes her in similar language:

You are beautiful as Tirzah, my love, comely as Jerusalem, terrible as an army with banners. Turn away your eyes from me, for they disturb me--- Your hair is like a flock of goats, moving down the slopes of Gilead. (Sol. 6:4 5)

Now you can see how figurative this language is. If any young swains were to take this literally today and try to pass this language along I am sure they would be misunderstood. But this is the impressionistic approach and there is beauty of expression here:

The Song of Solomon

Your teeth are like a flock of ewes that have come up from the washing, all of them bear twins, and not one among them is bereaved. (6:6) That means that she didn't have any missing. She had a full set and they had just been washed. Your cheeks are like halves of a pomegranate behind your veil. There are sixty queens and eighty concubines, and maidens without number. My dove, my perfect one, is only one, the darling of her mother, flawless to her that bore her. (6:7-9) Obviously, this is the language of love. The book 57 bes married love as God intended it to be. It is important to see that. For the full abandonment to one another in mutual satisfaction which is described in this book is possible only because it is experienced within that total oneness which only marriage permits. That is strongly emphasized throughout this book by a three-fold warning which the bride addresses to the unmarried girls---the chorus referred to as the daughters of Jerusalem. Three different times the bride, turning from her rapture and her delight with her love, gives these girls the secret of this delight: I adjure you, O daughters of Jerusalem...that you stir not up nor awaken love until it please. (Sol. 2:7; 3:5; 8:4) This is the secret of delight like this in marriage. What does she mean? She means, do not prematurely stimulate love. Wait until it develops on its own. Do not arouse it by artificial means before it is ready. Let it begin of itself in its own good time. It is monstrous to watch foolish and even fatuous mothers who encourage their children to ape adults in dancing and dating and petting even before they enter their teens. Why? Because they are trying to stir them up to adult activities, the activities of love, before their time.

It is like trying to open the bud before it is ready to open; you simply destroy it. We are seeing the results of much of this in our own society. For the young people who want the best in love, the greatest, the most this book teaches them to leave off petting and necking and so forth until they can say, as this bride says, He brought me to the banqueting house, and his banner over me was love. (Sol. 2:4) Or as the bridegroom says: Set me as a seal upon your heart, as a seal upon your arm; for love is strong as death, jealousy is cruel as the grave. Its flashes are flashes of fire, a most vehement flame. Many waters cannot quench love, neither can floods drown it...(Sol. 8:6-7) God has ordained that all these delights reflected here be a part of the experience of men and women, but only in the relationship which makes it possible, which is marriage. Therefore, this book is a powerful plea for chastity and purity in life until the time of marriage comes. But of course we have not heard the deepest message of this song until we pass behind the description of this purely physical human love, perfect as it is, to read it as an expression of communion between man and God, between Christ and his church. From the very earliest Christian centuries, this book was taken in that way. Even the Jews took it allegorically in that sense. The preface to this song in one of the Jewish books, or Targums, reads something like this: This is the Song of Solomon, the prophet king of Israel, which he sang before Jehovah the Lord.

The Song of Solomon

You see, he wasn't singing just a purely human love song. He sang this before Jehovah. This was a song about his own relationship to his God, and the early church fathers took it in that light. It was because of this interpretation that this song was such a comfort to the persecuted saints of the Reformation and the post-Reformation periods. Someone has well said, "If you love Jesus Christ, you will love this song because here are words that fully express the rapture of the heart that has fallen in love with Christ." When you read the book of Ecclesiastes, you read of man's search throughout the world for something to satisfy his heart, and the message of that book is simply that if a man gains the world it isn't enough. His heart is still empty because the heart is greater than its object. But the message of the Song of Solomon is that Christ is so tremendous, so mighty, and so magnificent, that the heart that has fallen in love with him will never be able to fully plumb the depths of his love and his concern and his care. The object, Christ, is greater than the heart. Every passage in this song, therefore, can be reverently lifted to this higher level of a heart enraptured with its Lord. Taken thus, it reveals a highly significant truth. It reveals that marriage is the key to human life. This is not to say that those who are not yet married should be discouraged by that. For regardless of whether you find marriage or not on the physical level, this is still true. What is marriage? Have you ever thought about marriage? About what lies behind the institution of marriage? It has been my privilege many times to marry people, and I have to deal with certain state laws. Marriage is not the product of human society. It is not something that people invented after they began to live together. Marriage goes back to the very

Sexual Healing In the Confines of Marriage

dawn of the human race. Marriage is an absolutely integral part of human life, and physical marriage, between man and wife, is simply a picture of a deeper relationship that is true of everyone. This principle is discussed in Romans 7, as the apostle Paul opens that great argument with an illustration of a married woman. While she is married, she is bound by the law to her husband. And if, while she is married to him, she falls in love with another man, she will gain the stigma of an adulteress, that is, she will expose herself as breaking the basic law of life. But if the husband dies, then she is free to be married to another man. (Rom. 7: 1-3). Why does he say all this? Because it is an illustration of what happens in the life of every one of us. Paul says we were married to the old life, to the old Adam. We were joined to an evil man. And that is the problem with human life. Man was made to be mastered and he simply cannot exist without a master. Every one of us has a master whether we like it or not. The whole story of the Bible is that it is either God who masters us or it is the devil. It is one or the other. Both Christ and the apostles make it very plain that the whole world, every man and every woman, is mastered by another force, either God or the devil. This is why Jesus said that no man can serve two masters. You can't give yourself to both of them. There must be a choice in life. Either you hate the one and love the other, or cling to one and separate from the other. You can't do both. So man must be mastered. In other words he is made for marriage since marriage is a picture of the mastery of one life by another. And this book says that the master who was made for man, the master that God intended for man to have. is the Lord Jesus Christ. Man mastered by Jesus enters into his fullness and glory, all that

The Song of Solomon

God intends for man. As you read in this book of the rapturous delight that the bride and the bridegroom experience in one another you are reading a magnificent and beautiful description of what God intends the relationship to be between himself and each individual. That is why the great commandment is, "You shall love the Lord your God with all your heart, and with all your soul, and with all your mind." (Matt. 22:37) That is the first and greatest commandment, for out of that flows everything else, including loving your neighbor as yourself. So this book is very important in that it deals with a very important relationship. In Christ we have the true bridegroom, and the church is his bride, as Paul puts it in Ephesians: Husbands, love your wives, as Christ loved the church and gave himself up for her..(Eph. 5:25) He goes on to describe the work of Chris 61 his church and then he says again: This is a great mystery, and I take it to mean Christ and the church. (Eph. 5:32) So the love of a husband and wife is a picture of the love of Christ and his church. In other words, the love of a husband and wife is simply a manifestation and a picture of that deeper love which is God's intention for human life. So in this book we have a picture of what God will fulfill in the heart and life of one who loves him. Listen to these beautiful words of the bridegroom to the bride: "For lo, the winter is past, the rain is over and gone. The flowers appear on the earth, the time of singing has come, and the voice of the turtledove is heard in our land. The fig tree puts forth its figs, and the vines are in blossom; they give forth fragrance. Arise, my love, my fair one, and come away." (Sol. 2:13) There is the springtime of life. But it doesn't lie in the past. It lies in the future.

Sexual Healing In the Confines of Marriage

One day this whole world will experience springtime like that. The Lord Jesus Christ, returning at last to claim his waiting bride, will greet her in words very much like those. The springtime will come, the time of singing, the time when earth shall blossom again and the curse will be lifted and the flowers will appear on the earth. This is a picture of what can take place in the heart of one who falls in love with Jesus Christ and enters into springtime. The cold winter of loneliness, misery, and selfishness is past and the time of singing has come. The Christian church was raised from a low, desolate condition, by the grace of Christ relied on. Believers, by the power of grace, are brought up from the wilderness. A sinful state is a wilderness in which there is no true comfort; it is a wandering, wanting state: There is no coming out of this wilderness, but leaning on Christ as our Beloved, by faith; not leaning to our own understanding, nor trusting in any righteousness of our own; but in the strength of him, who is the Lord our Righteousness. The words of the church to Christ which follow, entreat an abiding place in his love, and protection by his power. Set me as a seal upon your heart; let me always have a place in your heart; let me have an impression of love upon your heart. Of this the soul would be assured, and without a sense thereof no rest is to be found. Those who truly love Christ are jealous of everything that would draw them from him; especially of themselves, lest they should do anything to provoke him to withdraw from them. If we love Christ, the fear of coming short of his love, or the temptations to forsake him, will be most painful to us. No waters can quench Christ's love to us, nor do any floods drown it.

The Song of Solomon

Let nothing abate our love to him. Nor will life, and all its comforts, entice a believer from loving Christ. Love of Christ, will enable us to repel and triumph over temptations from the smiles of the world, as well as from its frowns. The bride says this as she clings to his arm and rests her head upon his bosom. Compare John 13:23; John 21:20. This brief dialogue corresponds to the longer one Cant. 4:7-5:1, on the day of their espousals. Allegorical interpreters find a fulfillment of this in the close of the present dispensation, the restoration of Israel to the land of promise, and the manifestation of Messiah to His ancient people there, or His Second Advent to the Church. The Targum makes Sol 8:6 a prayer of Israel restored to the holy land that they may never again be carried into captivity, and Sol 8:7 the Lord's answering assurance that Israel henceforth is safe.

Compare Isaiah 65:24; Isaiah 62:3-4. Songs 8:6 The key-note of the poem. It forms the Old Testament counterpart to Paul's panegyric 1 Corinthians 13:1-13 under the New. (a) Love is here regarded as a universal power, an elemental principle of all true being, alone able to cope with the two eternal foes of God and man, Death and his kingdom.

"For strong as death is love,

Tenacious as Sheol is jealousy."

"Jealousy" is here another term for "love," expressing the inexorable force and ardor of this affection, which can neither yield nor share possession of its object, and is identified in the mind of the sacred writer with divine or true life.

(b) He goes on to describe it as an all-pervading Fire, kindled by the Eternal One, and partaking of His essence:

"Its brands are brands of fire,

A lightning-flash from Jah."

Compare Deuteronomy 4:24.

(c) This divine principle is next represented as overcoming in its might all opposing agencies whatsoever, symbolized by water.

(d) From all which it follows that love, even as a human affection, must be reverenced, and dealt with so as not to be bought by aught of different nature; the attempt to do this awakening only scorn. 6. Implying approaching absence of the Bridegroom. His Holy Priesthood also in heaven (Ex 28:6-12, 15-30; Heb 4:14); "his heart" there answering to "your heart" here, and "two shoulders" to "arm." (Compare Jer. 22:24, with Hag 2:23). But the Holy Ghost (Eph 1:13, 14). As in So 8:5, she was "leaning" on Him, that is, her arm on His arm, her head on His bosom; so she prays now that before they part, her impression may be engraven both on His heart and His arm, answering to His love and His power (Ps 77:15; see Ge. 38:18; Isa 62:3). love is strong as death—(Ac 21:13; Ro 8:35-39; Re 12:11).

The Song of Solomon

This their love unto death flows from His (Jn. 10:15; 15:13). jealousy ... the grave—Zealous love, jealous of all that would come between the soul and Jesus Christ (1Ki 19:10; Ps 106:30, 31; Lu 9:60; 14:26; 1Co 16:22). cruel—rather, "unyielding" hard, as the grave will not let go those whom it once holds (Jn. 10:28). A most vehement flame—literally, "the fire-flame of Jehovah" (Ps 80:16; Isa 6:6). Nowhere else is God's name found in the Song. The zeal that burnt in Jesus Christ (Ps 69:9; Lu 12:49, 50) kindled in His followers (Ac 2:3; Ro 15:30; Php. 2:17). Set me as a seal upon your heart, as a seal upon your arm: these are undoubtedly the words of the bride. The sense is, Let thy mind and thy heart be constantly set upon me, let me be engraved upon the tables of your heart. He seems to allude to the engraved tablets which are frequently worn upon the breast, and to the signet on a man's arm or hand, which men prize at a more than ordinary rate, as appears from Jeremiah 22:24 Haggai 2:23, and which are continually in their sight. For love, my love to thee, from whence this desire proceeds, is strong as death; which conquers every living thing, and cannot be resisted nor vanquished. Jealousy, or zeal; my ardent love to thee, which also fills me with fears and jealousies, lest thou should bestow your affections upon others, and cool in thy love to me, or withdraw thy love from me; for true believers are subject to these passions.

Cruel, Heb. hard; grievous and terrible, and sometimes ready to overwhelm me, and swallow me up; and therefore have pity upon me, and do not leave me. Are coals of fire; it burns and melts my heart like fire. Set me as a seal upon your heart, as a seal upon your arm,.... These are still the words of the church, speaking to Christ as she walked along with him, as the affixes in the Hebrew text show; in which she desires to have a fixed abiding place in his heart; to continue firmly in his love, and to have further manifestations of it; to be always remembered and supported by him; to be ever on his mind, and constantly under his care and protection; and to have a full assurance of interest in his love, and in his power, which is the sealing work of his Spirit, Ephesians 1:13. The allusion seems to be to the high: priest, a type of Christ, who had the names of the children of Israel engraved on precious stones, and bore by him on his shoulders, and on his heart, for a memorial before the Lord continually; or to the names of persons, engraved on jewels, wore by lovers on their arms or breasts, or to their pictures put there; not to signets or seals wore on those parts, but to the names and images of persons impressed on them: the Ethiopians (p) understand it of something bound upon the arm, by which persons might be known, as was used in their country. The church's desire is, that she might be affectionately loved by Christ, be deeply fixed in his heart, be ever in his view, owned and acknowledged by him, and protected by the arm of his power.

The Song of Solomon

Her reasons follow:

for love is strong as death; that is, the love or the church to Christ, which caused her to make the above requests: death conquers all; against it there is no standing; such was the love of the church, it surmounted all difficulties that lay in the way of enjoying Christ; nothing could separate from it; she was conquered by it herself (q); and could not live without him; a frown, an angry look from him, was as death unto her; yea, she could readily part with life and suffer death for his sake; death itself could not part her from him, or separate him from her love (r); so that her love was stronger than death;

jealousy is cruel as the grave: the jealousy she had of Christ's love to her which was her weakness; and yet it was very torturing and afflicting, though at the same time it showed the greatness of her love to Christ: or "envy", that is of wicked men, she was the object of, which exceeds cruel wrath and outrageous anger, Proverbs 27:4; or rather her "zeal" (s), which is no other than ardent love for Christ his Gospel, cause, and interest; which ate up and consumed her spirits, as the grave does what is cast into it. Psalm 119:139 (t) gives the epithet of "cruel" to love; the coals thereof are coals of fire; which expresses the fervency of her love to Christ, and zeal for the honor of his name: which, though sometimes cold and languid, is rekindled, and becomes hot and flaming; and is, like fire, insatiable, one of the four things that say, "It is not enough", Proverbs 30:16; which has a most vehement flame; nothing is, nor, common with other writers (u), than to attribute flame to love, and to call it a fire; here a most vehement flame.

Sexual Healing In the Confines of Marriage

Or, "the flame of Jah" or "Jehovah" (w); an exceeding great one: the Hebrews use one or other of the names of God, as a superlative; so the mountains of God, and cedars of God, mean exceeding great ones; and here it expresses the church's love in the highest degree, in such a flame as not to be quenched, as follows: or it signifies, that the flame of love in her breast was kindled by the Lord himself (x), by his Spirit, compared to fire; or by his love, shed abroad in her heart by him, Hence it appears to be false, what is sometimes said, that the name of God is not used in this Song; since the greatest of all his names, Jab or Jehovah, is here expressed. As seals are not impressed upon the heart, nor upon the arm, we must understand here the ring seals which were bound round the neck with a cord (Genesis 38:18) and carried in the bosom, or which were worn on the finger (Jeremiah 22:24). This last passage interprets the bride's request. She wishes to be united in the closest way with her lover, and to be valued as his most precious possessions were valued. Haggai 2:23, perhaps rightly, would put for the second châthôm='seal,' some word like tsâmîdh, signifying a bracelet. Where the lover longs to be a jewel in his lady's ear: "It is the miller's daughter, And she is grown so dear, so dear, That I would be the jewel, That trembles in her ear." strong as death] Love is as irresistible as death, which none can escape. Jealousy is cruel as the grave] Jealousy is as unrelenting as Sheol, the place of the dead, from which none can ever escape; Proverbs 27:20. The meaning is that love and jealousy have irresistible power over those whom they bring under their sway.

The Song of Solomon

Her reference to jealousy would seem to shew that she fears the effect of her love upon herself, if he should not join himself indissolubly with her. The coals thereof are coals of fire] R.V. The flashes thereof are flashes of fire. Love glows and burns in the heart like flame. A most vehement flame] Heb, shalhebheth yâh, a flame of Jah, a flame of supernatural power, one that is kindled and cherished by God. Verses 6, 7. - Set me as a seal upon your heart, as a seal upon your arm: for love is strong as death; jealousy is cruel as the grave: the flashes thereof are flashes of fire, a very flame of the Lord. Many waters cannot quench love, neither can the floods drown it; if a man would give all the substance of his house for love, he would be utterly contemned. Is this to be regarded as the reply of the bride to the tender allusion of her husband to their first love; or is it, as some think, only the first words which belong to the bride, while the rest of the two verses are a kind of chorus echoing her loving appeal, and bringing the general action of the poem to a conclusion? It is difficult to decide this, and the meaning is not affected either way. Perhaps, however, it is best to take it as spoken by the bride, who continues her address to the end of the eighth verse. She is full of joy in the return of perfect confidence; she prays that the full tide of affection may never cease to flow, that there be no ebbing of that happy.

feeling in which she now delights; and then sings the praise of love itself, as though a prelude of praise to a long and eternal peace. The seal is the signet ring, chotham, from a root "to impress" It was sometimes carried by a string on the breast, and would, therefore, be near the heart (Genesis 38:18). It was sometimes worn on the hand (Jeremiah 22:24; and Genesis 41:42; Esther 3:12). It was not worn on the arm like a bracelet (2 Samuel 1:10). Probably it was not the signet ring which is referred to in the second clause: "Set me as a seal on your heart, and as a bracelet on your arm." The same simile is not infrequent in the prophets. The desire of Shulamith was to escape all possibility of those declensions of which she had spoken before. "Let me never be out of thy thoughts; let me never go back from my fullness of joy in thy love." The true believer understands well such language. He knows that the maintenance of devout affection is not a matter of mere desire and will. The Lord himself must help us with his blessed gifts, the influence of his gracious Spirit to overcome the feebleness and fickleness of a fallen heart. We want to be close to the heart of the Savior; we want to be constantly in his eye, and so diligently employed in his service, so closely associated with the work of his mighty arm, that we shall be ever receiving from him the signs and evidences of his approval and affection. The purity and perfection of true love are the theme of every sincere believer. The priceless value of such love is described in the Book of Proverbs (Proverbs 6:30), in Numbers 22:18, and 1 Corinthians 13:3. It is an unquenchable flame - nothing can resist it.

The Song of Solomon

We cannot but recall the rapturous language of one who himself was an example of the highest devotedness to the Savior, who rejoiced over death and the grave in the consciousness of victory through him from whose love nothing can separate us (Romans 8:38; 1 Corinthians 15:54). Certainly the history of the sufferings and trials of the true Church form a most striking commentary upon these words. Floods of persecution have swept over it, but they have not quenched love. The flame has burst forth again and again when it seemed to be extinguished, and it has become a very "flame of the Lord." The bush has been burning, but has not been consumed. By jealousy is intended love in its intensity not bearing arrival. The "flame of the Lord" may be compared with "the voice of the Lord," which is described in Hebrew poetry as connected with the fury of the storm. The flame, therefore, would be lightning and the voice thunder. The whole of this passage, which forms a kind of keynote of the poem, is more like a distinct strain introduced to give climax to the succession of songs than the natural expression of the bride's feelings. It has been always regarded as one of the sublimest apostrophes to love to be found anywhere. The enemies of God and of humanity are represented as falling before it, death and the grave. Its vehemence and force of manifestation are brought vividly before us by the comparison of the flash of lightning.

Sexual Healing In the Confines of Marriage

It is remarkable that this exaltation of love should be included in the Old Testament, thus proving that the Mosaic Law, with its formal prescriptions, by no means fulfils the whole purpose of God in his revelation to the world. As the New Testament would not have been complete without the message of the beloved disciple, so this Old Testament must have its song of love. Nor is it only the ideal and the heavenly love which is celebrated, but human affection itself is placed very high, because it is associated with that which is Divine. It is a more precious thing than mere wealth or worldly honor, and he that trifles with it deserves the utmost scorn and contempt of his fellows. It is well to remark how consistently the poetic framework is maintained. There is no attempt to leave the lines of human relations even at this point, whets evidently the sentiment rises above them. The love which is apostrophized is not removed from earth in order to be seen apart from all earthly imperfections and impurities. We are invited rather to look through the human to the Divine which embraces it and glorifies it. That. is the method of the Divine revelation throughout. "The Word was made flesh, and dwelt among us." We do not need to take Solomon's Song as an allegory. It is a song of human love, but as such it is a symbol of that which is Divine.

12 In the morning we will start for the vineyards,

    See whether the vine is in bloom,

    Whether the vine-blossoms have opened,

    The pomegranates budded -

The Song of Solomon

There will I give thee my love.

13 The mandrakes breathe a pleasant odor,

And over our doors are all kinds of excellent fruits,

New, also old,

Which, my beloved, I have kept for you.

MUTUAL LOVE. Song of Shulamith in the royal chambers. Chorus of ladies, daughters of Jerusalem. Verse 2. - Let him kiss me with the kisses of his mouth: for thy love is better than wine. Whether we take these words as put in the lips of the bride herself, or of the chorus as identifying themselves with her, is of little consequence. It is certain that the idea intended to be expressed is that of delight in the approach of the royal bridegroom. The future is used by choice, "Let me be taken up into the closest fellowship and embrace." The "kisses" must be interpreted in a figurative sense, or the sacred character of the whole book must be removed. The words may be rendered, with one of his kisses; the sweetness of his lips is such that one kiss would be rapture. Some have thought that allusion is intended to the custom among idolaters referred to in Job 31:27, "My mouth hath kissed my hand;" but the meaning is simply that of affection. The great majority of Christian commentators have regarded the words as expressive of desire towards God. Origen said, the Church of the old dispensation longing after higher revelations, as through the Incarnation, "How long shall he send me kisses by Moses and the prophets?

Sexual Healing In the Confines of Marriage

I desire the touch of his own lips." It is dangerous to attempt specific applications of a metaphor. The general truth of it is all that need be admitted. If the relation between God and his people is one that can be set forth under the image of human affection, then there is no impropriety in the language of Solomon's Song. "To kiss a kiss" is the ordinary Hebraic form ("to counsel a counsel"). Your love is better than wine. The plural is used, "loves," as in the word "life" the abstract for the concrete, perhaps in order to indicate the manifestation of love in many caresses. The change from the third person to the second is common in poetry. The comparison with wine may be taken either as denoting sweetness or exhilarating effects. The intoxicating power of wine is but rarely referred to in Scripture, as the ordinary wine was distinguished from strong drink. The Septuagint, altering the vowels of the word "love," turn it into "breasts," and must therefore have supposed it addressed to the bride. The word is connected with the Arabic, and runs through the languages, (Dada, Dido, David). Perhaps the reference to wine, as subsequently to the ointments, may be explained by the fact that the song is supposed to be sung while wine is presented in the chamber, and while the perfumes are poured out in preparation for the entrance of the royal bridegroom. We can scarcely doubt that the opening words are intended to be the utterance of loving desire on the part of the bride in the presence of the daughters of Jerusalem. Some have suggested that vers. 1-8 are from a kind of responsive dialogue, but the view of the older interpreters and others of the moderns, seems more correct, that all the first seven verses are in the mouth of Shulamith, and then ver. 8 comes in naturally as a chorus in reply to the song

The Song of Solomon

of the bride. The use of the plural, "We will run after thee," etc., is easily explicable. The bride is surrounded by her admiring companions and attendants. They are congratulating her on the king's love. She speaks as from the midst of the company of ladies. The Song of Songs, which is Solomon's, this is certainly the title of the book which follows, although in our present Hebrew Bible it is the first verse of the book preceded by the shorter form, 'The Song of Songs.' The Septuagint has simply the title Ασμα, So that our English title in the Authorized Version, 'The Song of Solomon,' has no ancient authority. It is well altered in the Revised Version to 'The Song of Songs.' The word "song" (שִׁיר) does not necessarily convey the meaning. composed to be sung to music, if the performance of the words were chiefly in view, the word would have been carmen, "lyric poem," "hymn," or "ode." The Greek Ασμα ἀσμάτων, and the Latin of the Vulgate, Canticum canticorum, accord with the Hebrew in representing the work as taking a high place either in the esteem of the Church or, on account of the subject, in the esteem of the writer. Luther expresses the same idea in the title he attaches to it, 'Das Hohelied,' that is, the chief or finest of songs. The reference may be to the excellence of the literary form, but probably that which suggested the title was the supreme beauty of the love which prompted the songs. The title may be regarded as applied to the whole book, or to the first portion of it giving the name to the whole. If it be a collection of separate songs strung together, as some think by mere resemblance in style and subject, then the words, "which is Solomon's" apply to the first song alone.

But the unity which is clearly to be traced through the book to the end makes it probable that the title is meant to ascribe the work to the authorship of Solomon. This is the opinion of the majority of critics. It must have come either from the wise king himself, or from some one of his contemporaries or immediate successors. The preposition is the lamedh auctoris. If the meaning were "referring to," another preposition would have been employed. It has been remarked by some that the absence of any description of Solomon as "King of Israel" or "son of David," as in Proverbs and Ecclesiastes, confirms the view that Solomon himself was the sole author. Some have argued against the authenticity of the title on the ground that the longer form of the relative, is used in it, whereas in the book itself the shorter form, is found, but no dependence, can be placed on that argument regarded by itself, for the same writer employs both forms, as Jeremiah, who uses the longer form in his prophecies and the shorter in Lamentations. The shorter form is, in fact, the elder, being Old Canaanitish or Phoenician, which is a lengthened form of, and afterwards became One writer however, holds that the relative pronoun as a substantive origin, and compares it with the Arabic it he and the Assyrian asar, meaning "track" or "place," like the German welcher, But whether this be so or not, it is certainly unsafe to date any book by the form found in it of the, relative pronoun. We know that in poetry the abbreviated form is common. It was probably a North Palestine provincialism, as we see in the Book of Kings. It became common in prose writings after the Captivity because of the degradation of Hebrew, but it was not unknown before that time either in prose or poetry.

The Song of Solomon

With regard to the exact description of the poetic form of the Song of Songs, the difference among critics is considerable, but the question is scarcely worth discussing. There undoubtedly is unity of conception in the songs which are brought together, but it cannot be of importance to prove that there is dramatic unity strictly speaking; there is no dramatic procedure, nor can we suppose that there is any ultimate aim at dramatic representation. But the Exposition which follows will suffice to show that there are facts of history in the background of the poem; if the suggestions of the language and scenery be followed, the facts are very beautiful and even romantic - the love of the great king for one of his own subjects, a lovely northern maiden, whose simplicity and purity of character are a great attraction and lend much force to the religious sentiment of the song. In 1 Kings 5:12 we read that "the Lord gave Solomon wisdom, as he promised him." That divinely inspired wisdom enabled him, notwithstanding his own personal errors, to idealize and sanctify the lovely episode of his life which lies at the foundation of his poem. And the Church of God in every age has appreciated, more or less widely, the inspiration, both of matter and of form, which breathed in it. We are told that Solomon composed one thousand and five songs (1 Kings 4:32); whether this is a part of that collection or not we cannot certainly say, but that it is a mere fasciculus, or collection of separate songs, strung together by their general erotic character, is what we cannot believe. No doubt, as one scholar has observed, the Arabian poets were accustomed to arrange their poems in what they compared to a string of pearls, but we can scarcely carry such a fact into the Bible, and deal with sacred books as mere literary remains. There must be a deep religious meaning in such language, and it is in accordance with Eastern usage that amatory songs should be so employed. What the meaning is we must persistently ask, and however much has been wrongly said in the past, while we believe in the Divine authority of the Old Testament we must not renounce the endeavor to find the Song of Songs worthy of its title and its place.

A Message From The Pastor's Desk

The world says date then marry; the Kingdom of GOD says marry then date. See there are so many rules and regulations that man has adopted in carrying out the sanctity of marriage. So many ideologies and leaning on one's own understanding along with what many have been taught to exercise marriage. In fact another factions being push to the forefront to redefine the sanctity of marriage is through the LGBT community. There philosophy is based on civil rights when simply there battle is a human right...a human right for a man and a man to marry as well as two women. The fact is the kingdom of GOD does not speak against a man and a woman having sex or any manner of companionship, GOD actually ordain this pleasure moments. This is the purpose for allowing this book of songs, The Song of Solomon to help "The Kingdom Man" and "The Kingdom Woman" to be informed of GODS thoughts of such pleasurable moments. These pleasurable moments are just exercise within the Sexual Healing in the Confines of Marriage.

THE KINGDOM CULTUREFELLOWSHIP MINISTRIES
&
CHRISTIAN SELF PUBLISHING CO.

THE KINGDOM CULTURE EXPLORATORY

STUDY BIBLE

THE KINGDOM ENGLISH STANDARD BIBLE

www.ingramcontent.com/pod-product-compliance
Lightning Source LLC
Chambersburg PA
CBHW022108160426
43198CB00008B/400